WHAT YOU NEED TO KNOW ABOUT STRATEGY

JO WHITEHEAD

CAPSTONE

658·4   529/431.

CONTENTS

Introduction	1
1 – What Is Strategy?	3
2 – From the Outside	37
3 – From the Inside	71
4 – Evolution	113
5 – Issues and Options	145
6 – The Priorities	183
7 – Process	209
8 – Engagement	245
On Your Way	277
Acknowledgements	281
Index	283

INTRODUCTION

The concept of business strategy was barely known or cared about before the 1970s, but these days most managers, whether they work in a small business, a not-for-profit organisation or a large company, want to know how to create strategy.

Although there are many books about strategy, relatively few describe *how* to create it. Some describe hot new strategies or important concepts; others are filled with dubious advice and quick fixes that may do more harm than good. But practical guidance on designing strategy is in short supply. Existing textbooks present, at best, a very idiosyncratic or incomplete view of how to do so.

This book aims to fill the gap, drawing on a career spent as a partner with the world's top strategy consulting firm and from teaching strategy at major business schools and companies. It integrates accepted research and thinking, while offering simple-to-use frameworks. In addition to the tools and concepts that managers need to know, it offers advice on how to involve the right people in a stimulating and challenging process.

This book does not pretend that devising a strategy is easy. Like anything else, to become an accomplished strategist requires practice. The website for the book, **www.whatyouneedtoknowaboutstrategy.com** provides case studies and examples that illustrate the application of the tools and techniques presented, as well as listing further materials, references and ideas. Suggestions for further reading are included at the end of each chapter.

Enjoy the book and start building your strategy skills!

CHAPTER 1

WHAT IS STRATEGY?

WHAT IT'S ALL ABOUT ➡

► What strategy is

► Why strategy is important

► The basic strategy questions

► Answering the questions

How do you develop a strategy? The answer is deceptively simple: you need to answer six basic strategy questions. But beware: each question has many possible answers and is beset with uncertainties. This chapter explains those six questions and the techniques and approaches available to answer them. Details of how to apply them are laid out in the chapters that follow.

But first you need to be clear about what strategy is and why being able to develop a sound strategy is important.

WHAT STRATEGY IS

Strategy is both the goal of an organisation, and the pathway it follows to achieve that goal.

Organisations have past, current and future strategies. This book is aimed at helping the reader design *future* strategies. Understanding past and current strategies is part of the design process but it is not the objective here.

Organisations are shaped by a mix of intended and unintended strategies. While the perspective of this book recognises the importance of considering and responding to the impact of unforeseen events, the goal is to help you design *intended* strategies – even if these need to be continually revised and refined in the light of new developments. In Benjamin Franklin's words, this book will help 'drive thy business'.

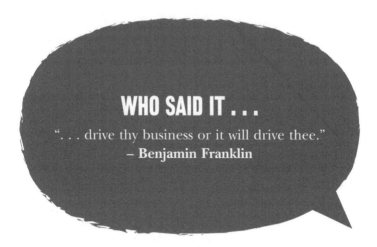

WHO SAID IT . . .

". . . drive thy business or it will drive thee."
– **Benjamin Franklin**

All intended strategies are decisions, but not all decisions create strategies. A strategic decision is one that is *difficult, hard to reverse,* and involves the commitment of *significant* resources.

For example, a manufacturing business has to decide how to lower costs by £50 million. If doing so will have a major impact on the cost structure and involve tricky choices – such as whether to cut costs in the current production facility, outsource production or build a new factory in a low cost location – then it could be described as a strategic decision. If the choice is relatively simple – such as switching to a more modern and well-tested production technology – then it is not.

What is 'strategic' depends on the perspective of those involved. For example, the head of the purchasing department may have to achieve savings of £10 million of the total £50 million target. The manager within the purchasing department who is in charge of purchasing energy may have the strategic goal of cutting costs by £1 million. The £50 million, £10 million and £1 million targets may all be strategic goals from the perspective of the individuals responsible for achieving them.

Strategy-making is relevant for many types of organisation. It is not exclusive to large corporations; smaller businesses or business units also have strategies. In this book we focus primarily on developing strategy for organisations that operate in competitive marketplaces. These may include not-for-profit organisations, many of which 'compete' in the market for supporters, donations and funding. There is also relevant material here for managers designing strategy for a function or department, as well as for those who do not operate in competitive markets, and even for individuals who want to develop a personal strategy.

Strategy is defined not just by the commitments involved, but also by the general direction of the pathway to be followed – the opportunities to be pursued. It is also defined by what is NOT done – by the constraints imposed on the pathway. For example, Apple's strategy for the iPod could be to maintain market share above 60% (the goal) in the MP3 player market (the opportunity) through continuous investment in product upgrades (a commitment of resources), while still delivering profit margins of at least 25% (a constraint).

Developing strategy involves three stages: realising a strategic decision is required, making the strategic decision, and implementing it. The main focus of this book will be on how to make the strategic decision. Each of the other stages requires a book of its own.

To summarise: strategy, as defined here, consists of an intended, future goal and the pathway to reach that goal. Creating strategy involves making difficult decisions about the opportunities to be targeted, the commitment of significant resources, and the constraints on the ways those resources can be used. Various levels in the organisation can each have a strategy, creating a cascading and coordinated set of goals and pathways.

WHY STRATEGY IS IMPORTANT

There are a number of reasons why developing a sound strategy is important.

Strategy can make a huge difference to the fate of an organisation. If a good strategy can transform a company – as the example of Steve Jobs and Apple overleaf illustrates – a bad one can kill it. Consider the following:

In 2008, **Lehman Brothers** was on the verge of bankruptcy. It had over-invested in the US property market and had virtually no equity to absorb the losses that would result from the downturn in the financial markets. But the management team – CEO Dick Fuld in particular

WHO YOU NEED TO KNOW
Steve Jobs

Apple CEO Steve Jobs is an iconic example of a leader of an organisation who is also its primary strategist. Not all leaders play this role; some rely heavily on other senior executives, senior staff or external advisers. But Jobs has repeatedly shaped the destinies of the organisations that he has led.

Under his leadership, Apple developed the Macintosh computer – to date, the only serious rival to the PC. He was forced out of Apple, only to bounce back as the owner and CEO of Pixar, a small animation company he acquired from George Lucas (who needed the money to help pay for his divorce). Pixar grew to be a leader in its field before selling out to Disney. By then, Jobs was back at Apple, which he rescued from a critical condition to become the creator of the iPod, iPhone and iPad – and a star of the global economy.

The development of the iPod is an interesting example of how strategy is often formed through a mixture of the intended, and the unintended. It was Jobs, with his knowledge of the Los Angeles-based film and music business acquired during his time at Pixar, who developed the goal of entering the music business – a direction that a Northern Californian computing company such as Apple would not normally have taken. But Jobs always sought to position the businesses he led at the forefront of the industry. He liked to quote ice hockey star Wayne Gretzky: 'I skate to where the puck is going to be, not where it is.'

Having set the goal, Apple then took a circuitous and opportunistic pathway to reach it. First, it acquired the technology to create digital music from a company called Soundjam, which had developed a superior way to create MP3 files that could be used to store music. iTunes was launched in 2001 as a way to download MP3 and CD files to the Mac. Following a chance visit by an independent consultant, who had an idea for creating a new and innovative MP3 player, Apple created the iPod. Jobs then exploited his connections with the music industry and the industry's paranoia about file-sharing websites such as Napster, to launch the iTunes Music Store website in 2003, selling MP3 files over the internet. Looking back, it all seems to add up, whereas in fact the pathway to the intended goal evolved over time, in response to unforeseen circumstances.

– failed to recognise the danger inherent in the current situation. He rejected offers to be acquired by foreign banks. He pushed to be rescued under conditions that suited him and Lehman rather than recognising that any deal that could save the bank was worth considering. Even as the US government moved in to force a final resolution of the problem, Fuld held to his uncompromising position. Lehman collapsed.

But the collapse was not inevitable. In the same context, John Thain, CEO of Merrill Lynch, recognised the reality of the situation and saw that his bank might be the next to go. He pulled off a quick merger with Bank of America that saved Merrill and gave its shareholders a great deal, given the circumstances.

In the 1990s, **Motorola** was a major competitor in the mobile phone business. At the time, competitors such as Nokia and Ericsson had begun shifting from analogue to digital technologies. Motorola had some of the key capabilities for digital in-house, and could have moved quickly to build a strong position in digital mobile telephony. But management decided that digital was not a significant opportunity and ignored it. This proved to be the beginning of the company's demise as a major player. Meanwhile, Nokia and Ericsson got it right and subsequently became the two top global competitors.

The **UK motorcycle industry** in the 1960s was the country's third-largest dollar export earner after cars and whisky. But the major manufacturers, such as Triumph, BSA and Norton, failed to recognise the threat posed by Japanese new entrants. They saw their objective as making racing bikes that would appeal to a niche market of enthusiasts. Meanwhile, Honda, Yamaha and Suzuki invested to grow the market. They saw biking as a potential pastime for everyone, and developed recreational bikes that were reliable and fun to ride. Ultimately, they used the scale developed from colonising the 'low end' of the market to develop fast bikes that eclipsed even the UK manufacturers' best machines. The latter went bankrupt, while the Japanese became global leaders. The UK companies saw the primary issue as how to get cash out of a declining niche business, and paid out high levels of dividends. The Japanese saw the issue as how to grow, and re-invested their profits in new models.

Organisations are having to revise their strategies more often. Over the last 20 years, markets have deregulated and competition has globalised. The internet has broken up established businesses, creating new competitors and more informed customers. Economic cycles continue to weed out the weak and test even the strong. Climate change and rising commodity prices challenge long-held business practices. All these phenomena create a continual pressure to reconsider even a winning formula. Change creates opportunity, but only to the organisation ready to revise and reformulate its strategy.

Strategy-making is a skill that is needed by more people, more of the time. Ideas about how strategy is developed have changed over the past few decades. At one time strategy was seen as being the responsibility of the leader. Then it was seen as the domain of corporate planning departments and specialist consultants.

Today we understand that strategy should not just be made by the CEO or strategy specialists. Strategy-making can involve a wide range of people from across the business: those who lead corporations develop corporate strategy, business unit heads develop business strategy, functional heads devise functional strategies, and departmental heads departmental strategies. Analysts may

WHO SAID IT . . .

"Effective strategists are not people who abstract themselves from the daily detail, but who immerse themselves in it while being able to abstract the relevant messages from it."
– **Henry Mintzberg**

support the process, but leaders and their teams are expected to devise and take ownership of their strategy. Further down the organisation, a range of people and teams may be involved in innovating, developing, refining and communicating the strategy. This is a welcome shift. Leaders who understand their organisation, markets and competitors *should* be in charge of making decisions about strategy, and those involved in the business should be able to contribute to strategic thinking.

Even if you are not involved directly in the design process, understanding your organisation's strategy is crucial to be effective in your job. To get ahead you need to show that you can take individual initiative and contribute to the success of the organisation as a whole. You need to know that your decisions are aligned with the goals and objectives of the organisation and how it intends to achieve them. Even if your organisation is not actively changing its strategy, or if you are not involved in designing strategy, you must be familiar with the language and logic of strategic thinking.

THE BASIC STRATEGY QUESTIONS

Having described the importance of strategy, we now turn to the heart of the matter: *How* do you come up with a strategy?

The answer is seemingly straightforward. Strategy design involves coming up with robust answers to the following six basic questions:

The strategy questions

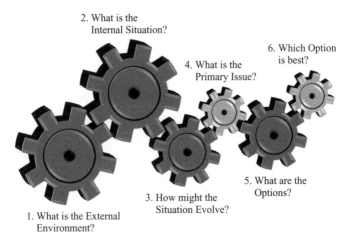

2. What is the Internal Situation?

6. Which Option is best?

4. What is the Primary Issue?

5. What are the Options?

3. How might the Situation Evolve?

1. What is the External Environment?

What Is the External Environment?

Strategy involves aligning the organisation's capabilities and assets with external opportunities and threats – so describing the external environment is a good place to start. However, this can be difficult to do, particularly when an organisation is facing rapid change or entering a new market.

For example, Honda famously misunderstood the US motorcycle market when it first entered it. It knew that there was a market for large bikes and tried to sell its most powerful machines – but these models proved to be unreliable in the US, where the average journey was much longer than on crowded Japanese roads. It was only when customers started to ask whether they could buy the smaller 50 cc bikes that Honda managers were riding as work vehicles that they realised that this was an untapped market. Even then, senior management took some persuading.

What is the Internal Situation?

Two aspects of the internal situation must be understood: the objectives of the organisation and its capabilities. The tricky part is that both have to be viewed in the context of the external environment. It is not enough to know that you have capabilities in R&D; you must understand how valuable they could be in generating superior products for customers and how these capabilities compare with those of your competitors.

How Might the Situation Evolve?

Your strategy will play out in an uncertain future. Understanding the current external environment and internal situation is an important start, but it is not enough. It is vital to project how things might evolve and identify the greatest sources of uncertainty. Is it the actions of competitors? Is it the way that the market will develop? Is it how your organisation will respond to change and a new direction? Your strategy should be robust and adaptable enough that it does not automatically fail in the face of unforeseen events. Expect the unexpected! This is one of the great challenges of strategy: you place big bets when you do not fully know the odds.

What is the Primary Issue?

Successful strategies tend to result from resolving a difficult issue in a way that is novel and hard for competitors to copy. Therefore defining the primary issue is a key step. When Apple entered the music business, for example, it identified the issue as how to help consumers to easily buy and play music.

The primary issue may seem obvious in hindsight but not be so at the time. Indeed, it is often redefined during the creation of a new strategy in a way that offers new insight and opens up new options. For Honda in the US motorcycle market, the initial issue was how to sell big, fast bikes in competition with US and European competitors. Later, it was redefined as how to develop the market for small motorbikes – but only after a long period of failing to build market share in the initial target segment.

What Are the Options?

Once the issue has been properly defined, options need to be identified. In the case of Apple, these were not clear. Even after defining the issue as how to enable consumers to easily access music, it took time to develop the iPod and the iTunes website. In the case of Honda it was a little clearer; once the issue had been redefined as how to develop the market for small motorbikes, the main options – such as a distribution channel and product design – became relatively easy to identify.

Which Option Is Best?

At some point an option has to be selected. In the case of Apple and Honda, a number of smaller decisions led to the overall shift in strategy. In other cases, such as when a major acquisition is required, there may be one big decision that needs particularly careful analysis and evaluation.

Since these questions are so important, it may be helpful to use the acronym EIEIO as an easy way to remember them. **E**xternal Environment, **I**nternal situation, how the

Alternative words and phrases

Words and phrases used in this Book	Alternative words and phrases commonly used
External and Internal environment	Situation assessment, Starting position, Context, Where we are today, Complexity
External environment	Market, Competitive environment, Industry, Micro-economics, Competitors, Customers, Customer needs, Opportunities, Threats
Objectives (part of the internal environment)	Aims, Goals, Ambitions, Vision, Mission, Stakeholder needs
Internal environment	Capabilities, Resources, Assets, Strengths, Weaknesses
Evolution (of the situation)	Change, Trends, Key uncertainties, Unknowns, Timeframes, Scenarios
Primary issue	Challenge, Difficulty, Complication, Obstacles, Complexities, Compromises, Opportunities
Options	Alternatives, Actions, Choices
Which option is best?	Evaluation, Assessment, Criteria, Probability, Decision

situation will **E**volve, the primary **I**ssue, and what the **O**ptions are.

The table above lists some of the alternative words and phrases that capture the ideas which are commonly used to describe the process of creating strategy. This may be helpful in establishing how the approach described here differs or is similar to how you think about strategy.

ANSWERING THE QUESTIONS

The questions may be simple but getting the correct answer is not, as the stories of Lehman Brothers, Motorola and the UK motorcycle industry illustrate. Even the best management teams can struggle, including those that eventually get it right. Apple took several years – having identified that it wanted to enter the music business – to come up with a successful way of doing so. Honda struggled to sell its big bikes in the US and only switched to selling smaller bikes when customers started asking for them. Clearly the answer was not immediately obvious.

One of the challenges in answering the strategy questions is the nature of the task itself, which is often misunderstood. Strategy-making does not conform to the stereotype of a logical, sequential, mechanical process, starting with the collection of data defined by standard templates which, like a sausage machine, spits out a fully-formed strategy at the end of it. Unlike the stereotype, it cannot be learned in the same way as the operation of a complex piece of machinery – simply by getting to grips with standard operating procedures and routines.

A more realistic notion is that of 'crafting strategy', as described by Henry Mintzberg, a professor at McGill University. Mintzberg compares creating strategy to the way a potter shapes a pot on the wheel; it is partly the application of a learned skill and partly an intuitive response to the nature of the situation and the emerging results. Good ideas sometimes turn out badly but give rise to new learning and opportunities – the very act of making the pot improves the skill of the potter.

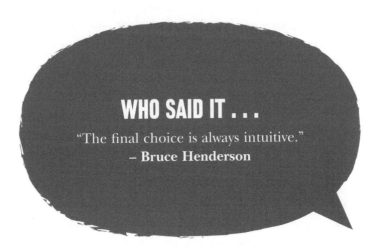

WHO SAID IT . . .

"The final choice is always intuitive."
– Bruce Henderson

The development of a good strategy is a creative act, often decided under high levels of uncertainty. The whole process involves a mix of analysis, judgment, gut feeling, opportunism, and trial and error. So a skilled strategist has to be a structured yet flexible thinker, deeply engaged in the situation they are evaluating, as well as dispassionately objective. This blend of ability is often described as a 'strategic mindset'.

What follows are some tips on how to design strategy based on this view.

Use a Mix of Approaches to Answer the Questions

Imagine you have defined a particular strategy question to focus on. For example, 'What are our options?' To answer the question, several approaches should be combined: intuition, data and analysis, strategy concepts, strategy tools or frameworks, and people and processes, as summarised in the following exhibit.

Four approaches to answering the questions

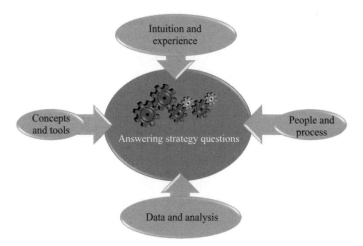

Intuition informed by relevant experience is a powerful way to answer the questions. The problem is that past experience is often not adequate for making strategic decisions about an evolving future. Lehman had to design strategy in the face of a developing financial crisis, Motorola had to design strategy for a new technology, and the UK motorcycle industry had to deal with a new type of competitor. Intuition based on experience would

have helped, but would not have been sufficient to come up with the right choice.

Data and analysis can fill in the gaps in our knowledge. For example, analysing the potential impact of a financial crash might have alerted Lehman management earlier to the risks inherent in their strategy. But the real challenge is to work out what data is required and how it should be analysed. Many organisations do not lack access to information, but they lack the ability to focus on the right information and to interpret it. Lehman was aware of the state of the financial markets, but did not use that information correctly. Data and analysis can be helpful but only if the individuals involved know how to use them properly. For this, strategic concepts and tools are invaluable.

A strategic concept is an idea that defines the nature of a successful strategy. For example, according to the concept of 'segmentation', competition occurs within particular segments of a market or industry, rather than at the level of the overall industry. For example, Moët & Chandon is part of the drinks industry, but competes in the segment for premium champagnes rather than against Coca Cola and Pepsi. Competitive battles are fought at the segment rather than the industry level.

Another example of a strategic concept is that of 'competitive advantage' – the idea that strategic and economic success comes not from being *good* but from being *better* than the competition. Moët & Chandon's success comes not from how good its marketing is, but how good it is *relative* to competing brands such as Taittinger and Veuve Cliquot.

Strategy concepts are helpful in framing the way you answer the questions. For example, consider how Moët & Chandon could use the concepts of segmentation and competitive advantage to address the question 'What are the options?' They would guide Moët to seek options that provide them with a competitive advantage in particular segments – for example, by building its market share further in premium champagnes. Extensions into other segments – other wines or other luxury goods, for example – might be feasible, but only if the Moët brand or its capabilities in brand management allowed it to outperform the established competitors in those segments.

Strategic concepts help define what data to gather and how to analyse it. For example, the concepts of segmentation and competitive advantage might suggest surveying potential customers in new business segments to see if they would prefer a Moët-branded product more than those of existing competitors, or investigating whether Moët's channels of distribution could be used for the new product.

An understanding of strategy concepts is fundamental to strategy. Later chapters will describe the most important ones, including segmentation, industry attractiveness, value creation, competitive advantage, mission and objectives, uncertainty, and engagement. However, for someone who is new to strategy they may seem rather abstract and difficult to apply.

Strategy tools or frameworks allow for a more structured approach to using the concepts – a more concrete way of structuring your thinking and analysis. There are many popular tools or frameworks, such as SWOT, key success factors, core competencies, scenario planning, value chain, five forces, industry life cycle, PESTLE and portfolio matrices. All of these, and more, are covered in subsequent chapters.

The most useful strategy tools are based on one or more strategy concepts. For example, a SWOT analysis requires you to lay out the strengths, weaknesses, opportunities and threats facing the organisation. Strengths and weaknesses are based on the concept of competitive advantage, while opportunities and threats are based on the concept of market attractiveness. Whether you use strategy concepts or more concrete tools and frameworks, you are drawing on the same set of fundamental ideas about what makes a strategy successful.

The decision to use strategy tools or strategy concepts will depend partly on how experienced you are in strategy. If you are relatively inexperienced it may be easier to use a strategy tool because it provides a more structured way of thinking through the answers to the questions. As you gain more familiarity with strategy, you will switch to using just the concepts in a more intuitive fashion. Do enough strategy and you won't even think about the concepts and frameworks you are using to assess situations and come up with options.

Strategy tools and frameworks are also helpful for holding a group discussion and in making presentations about the logic used during the strategy-making process.

Unfortunately, strategy concepts and tools alone will rarely get you to the right answer. Strategic decisions are almost always difficult, requiring experience and judgement. One individual rarely has the necessary breadth of experience to make a judgment on their own. Moreover, preconceptions and biases can lead even experienced experts into making a misjudgement.

People and process. Because strategy can rarely be designed by a single individual, bringing together the right people in an effective process is critical to answering strategy questions. In some cases, relatively few people can be involved and the process can be very simple, but, as we demonstrate later, it can be important to widen out strategy thinking across the organisation. A strategy process involving a mix of people with different expertise and perspectives, all willing to debate and challenge, is as essential to crafting strategy as finding the right strategy tool. It will engage the broader organisation in a debate, help answer the questions, and provide a platform of shared understanding from which to launch a successful roll-out.

Chapters 2 to 5 describe how to apply the concepts and tools to the intellectual process of answering the questions. The remaining chapters turn to the topics of people and process.

Make Sure You Work on the Right Question

Open some strategy textbooks and you will find flow diagrams showing how to develop a strategy using a logical sequence of steps, each of which involves answering a set of questions. In this model it is obvious when to move on to the next stage. In reality, almost all decision makers and decision-making processes dance around between different questions. Knowing which question you should be working on is part of the art of strategy-making.

Why does the strategy process not follow a typical pathway? Partly because the answer to some of the questions may already be known or answered intuitively, allowing the process to jump ahead to the more challenging and critical questions. Alternatively, the answer to certain questions may make the strategist revisit questions that they thought that they had already answered. For example, when Apple realised that producing an MP3 player was an interesting way to get into the music business, they would have revisited the question 'What is the external environment in the MP3 market'? to further evaluate existing MP3 products and competitors.

Another reason is that our brain is not wired to go through each question in order; it jumps creatively to conclusions, coming back only when it hits a problem. A team of senior managers will find it frustrating to be forced to go through a very rigid process, and this is unlikely to be an effective way of using their experience and insight. Different ways to sequence the strategy questions are discussed in Chapter 6.

This is why the questions in the earlier figure are depicted as a set of linked gear wheels rather than a one-way process. When you think about the answer to one question, it will make you consider other questions. As one wheel turns, it sets others in motion.

Be Selective About the Analysis Required

As mentioned above, some questions are likely to be easy to answer from experience and need less analysis. Others are more tricky and need to be explored in considerable depth. The important thing is to know when to probe to a high level of detail and when to move on.

For example, when evaluating the external environment there are many ways to spend your (limited) time. You could interview lots of customers, seeking to understand how their needs vary and whether any major segments are currently under-served. Or you could spend weeks evaluating competitors or even a particular aspect of a single competitor, such as its new product development process. Knowing where to direct your main efforts is essential.

The answer is to use a 'T' approach, using two types of analysis. For questions where you are pretty sure you know the answers, collect enough information to ensure that you are not deluded (interviewing outsiders is a good place to start). This broad but shallow level of analysis is represented by the horizontal bar at the top of the T. The vertical bar of the T represents the more detailed 'deep dive' – the intensive data collection and analysis you will need to answer critical issues where you are unsure or where there are competing viewpoints.

To know where to go deep, think of areas where you don't have enough experience to rely on intuition. For example, if you are a sales director you may understand your customers very well but be relatively ignorant of the cost structure of your competitors. Knowing where to focus is also a matter of thinking ahead to the main decisions that your strategy process has to make. Put the most effort into the questions that will have the most impact on your decision between options.

For example, Epson, the Japanese printer manufacturer, wanted to learn how to compete more effectively with Hewlett Packard. They commissioned a study of Hewlett Packard's product development process because they believed that the differences in this process were what differentiated between the companies, and thus where changes needed to be made.

If you are still unsure of where to focus your analytical efforts, lay out your argument and look for the main assumptions on which your conclusion depends. A good tool to do this is the Minto Pyramid Principle, shown in the following diagram. Focus your data collection and analysis on testing and supporting the key assumptions – described in the exhibit as 'Key line ideas'.

The Minto Pyramid Principle

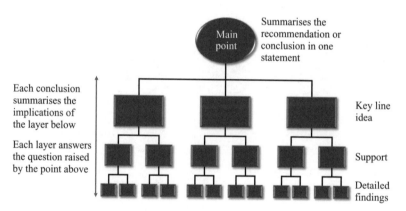

Expect the Unexpected

Coming up with a strategy to deal with the current situation can often seem overwhelming, but it is only part of the strategist's task. It is important to expect the unexpected and to design your strategy accordingly.

WHO YOU NEED TO KNOW
Barbara Minto

Barbara Minto holds an MBA from Harvard Business School, attending in only the second year in which women were accepted. She then worked at McKinsey & Company for ten years, having been hired as their first female consultant. She now runs her own consultancy, Minto International.

It was at McKinsey that she developed the 'Minto Pyramid Principle' as a way of structuring the communication of any complex message. The influence of this approach has spread far and wide, informing the strategic thinking of many.

The idea of the Minto Pyramid Principle is that a message should have one major conclusion or recommendation that is supported by a number of ideas grouped below it. Each of these 'key line' supporting points can itself be supported by a number of sub-points containing more detailed data and analysis. Any idea at any level always raises a question (how? or why?)

that is answered by the ideas on the
line below.

Not only can pyramiding be an effective method
of building and communicating an argument, it is
also a useful way of thinking through how much
detail is required to answer a particular question.
For example, early on in the strategy design
process, lay out what you think is the main
argument so that you can spot what key pieces of
information and analysis would best support and
test it. If one of the key line points of your
pyramid has no supporting data, you will know to
focus your efforts on supplying the detail.

The ability to think in a structured way is a useful
skill for the strategist. Without it, the ambiguity
and uncertainty involved in strategic analysis can
be overwhelming. With it, you can structure,
analyse, solve and communicate even the most
complex issues.

The skills that Barbara Minto has so effectively
taught and communicated over the past 40 years
have provided as much support to the
development of strategic thinking as the works of
leading academics and practitioners.

Because it is impossible to fully predict the future, good strategies incorporate planning for how to respond to events as they unfold. As this happens, new opportunities and threats emerge as well as the need for further decisions. Strategy is typically composed of a sequence of decisions rather than one big decision.

One approach to dealing with this is for the strategy to be flexible and include enough capacity to respond to unpredicted and unpredictable events. Some strategies even use a 'test-and-learn' approach – building in a capability to respond to the unexpected and evolve from there.

Supermarket chain Tesco, for example, developed a computer and logistics system that enabled it to respond

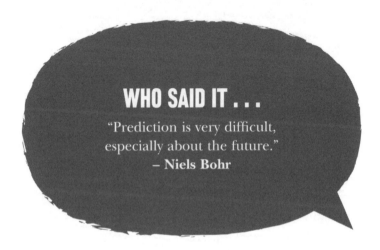

WHO SAID IT . . .

"Prediction is very difficult,
especially about the future."
– Niels Bohr

rapidly to changes in customer demand, allowing it to out-perform its competitors by offering better stocked shelves with popular products at competitive prices.

How uncertainty impacts on the strategy design will be discussed later in this book, but the general point to bear in mind is that you should never be fooled into thinking you can predict the future.

Practice, Practice, Practice!

By now it should be clear that, while there are plenty of tools, tips and techniques that can help, developing strategy is a complex skill to master. It is not enough to know how to do it in theory. Strategy-making, like anything else, takes practice. But major changes in strategy are not common, so getting practice can be difficult.

One of the goals of this book is to not only reveal the secrets of creating a strategy but to give the reader a chance to test and develop their skills. Multiple examples are provided to illustrate the concepts and tools described. A case study is available on the book's website, which also provides short tests, and further reading and web links are suggested at the end of each chapter.

Thinking about the way these ideas would apply to your own situation is an invaluable way to develop your skills. Even thinking through what a newspaper or magazine article says about strategy can be helpful in grounding ideas about strategy in reality.

In the end, with strategy as with so much else, only practice makes perfect, but this book will give you the initial understanding, tools, techniques and tips to get started.

WHAT YOU NEED TO READ

▶ Michael Porter provides a view of what strategy is and why it is important in 'What Is Strategy?' in the *Harvard Business Review*, November/December 1996, pp. 61-78.

▶ For other examples of strategy as a (similar) set of questions, see Richard Koch's *The Financial Times Guide to Strategy*, Pearson, 2006 or Jack Welch in the strategy section at www.welchway.com.

▶ Henry Mintzberg draws a powerful analogy between the nature of making strategy and making a pot in *Crafting Strategy*, Harvard Business Review, July-August 1987.

▶ *Building a Strategy Toolkit*, by Paula Jarzabkowski, Monica Giulietti, and Bruno

Oliveira, www.aimresearch.org, provides a useful summary of commonly used strategy tools.

▶ Strategy concepts are covered in many strategy textbooks. One of the best is Robert Grant's *Contemporary Strategy Analysis*, John Wiley & Sons Ltd, 2010.

▶ For a history of the development of the key concepts in strategy, see *Lords of Strategy* by Walter Kiechel III, Harvard Business Press, 2010.

IF YOU ONLY REMEMBER ONE THING

Strategy involves answering some difficult questions using intuition, data, concepts, tools, people and process.

CHAPTER 2

FROM THE OUTSIDE

WHAT IT'S ALL ABOUT

► The importance of segmenting the industry

► The concept of industry attractiveness

► The macro forces that shape industries

An organisation does not operate in a vacuum. Any strategy has to fit with the characteristics of its external environment, so let's begin from the outside. Given that multiple aspects of the environment could be evaluated – customers, markets, competitors, regulations, societal trends – where should you start? Clearly, a certain amount of data is needed to familiarise yourself with the environment, but how much should you collect?

Focus on data that answer a few basic questions about the environment:

1. *What industry are we in?* Before diving into a detailed assessment it's important to define what industry segment you are in. This often turns out to be more difficult than you might think.

2. *How attractive is it?* The opportunities offered by the industry will have a big impact on how successful an organisation can be. Some industries are so attractive that just being in them is enough to make a firm successful. Others are so tough that only one or two competitors make adequate returns.

3. *What is the broader context?* It is increasingly important for strategists to understand the broader context in which their organisation is competing. The attractiveness of a business and what it takes to be successful in it are influenced by broad trends such as climate change, chang-

ing government policies, and the emergence of new consumer concerns and pressure groups.

Answering these questions to flesh out your starting position can take time, but it is often where a lot of the heavy lifting is done – the 95% of a decision that is perspiration rather than inspiration. Fortunately there is a host of approaches, frameworks and tools to help.

WHO SAID IT . . .

"The essence of formulating competitive strategy is relating a company to its environment."
– Michael Porter

DEFINING INDUSTRY BOUNDARIES

Organisations operate in distinct environments. Barclays Bank does not operate in the same business environment as Ford. Economists call these 'industries' – the environments within which a set of collaborators and competitors pursue their activities. In general, industries include a number of competitors, although a few are monopolies. Industries can be populated by not-for-profit organisations, for example, charities which compete for funds. What it takes to win will vary from one industry to another – the rules of the game for banking are different to those for the car industry.

WHO SAID IT . . .

". . . the key aspect of the firm's environment is the industry or the industries in which it competes."
– **Michael Porter**

However, it can be difficult to define the boundaries of an industry. Where does one industry stop and a new one begin? In the car industry, which is used as an example throughout this chapter, the rules of the game are different for luxury cars, small cars, MPVs (multi-purpose vehicles), SUVs (sports utility vehicles), family saloons and vans. They also vary by country – the Chinese market is different from the US market. In fact, the car industry could be seen as many different industries, albeit with some common features.

At this point, let's explore our first strategy concept: segmentation.

SEGMENTATION

Segmentation involves dividing up an industry into sub-industries, each of which is different on one or more of the following key dimensions:

1. The growth rate.
2. The inherent profitability.
3. What it takes to win – sometimes described as 'sources of competitive advantage' or 'rules of the game'.

Segmentation is a critical first step in analysing the external environment because if you don't know the industry you are in it is impossible to begin to create a sensible strategy.

For example, if you were asked to describe the car business overall you might think (considering the above dimensions) that the growth rate was low, the inherent profitability was low (due to it being cyclical and competitive) and that the rules of the game were to be a low-cost, global giant like Toyota, Ford or Volkswagen. But the

SUV business in the US was, until recently, both fast growing and highly profitable. And winning in this segment required a US rather than a global presence. So if a car manufacturer only evaluated the industry at the level of 'cars', it would overlook the major differences between what was happening in the SUV segment vs. the car industry in general.

Segmentation is not only useful for analysing your current business, it can also be a creative activity, leading to new insights that improve existing strategies or even give rise to whole new businesses. For example, consider the insurance business. Traditionally this was segmented along product lines, such as motor vs. household insurance. But it can also be segmented by sales channel, e.g. via a sales force, via agents, either direct or through comparison websites. Growth rates, profitability and what it takes to win often vary more across channels than across products.

The insight that insurance can be segmented by channel has made it possible to create completely new types of insurance company. For example, Direct Line, became the first UK insurance company to use the telephone as their main channel of communication. Starting in 1985 with 65 employees, it now employs 10,000 people and is the recognised industry leader. More recently, the emergence of another new channel, price comparison websites, has allowed new insurance companies to set up with very low overheads, selling insurance at low prices. Segmenting by channels is now recognised as one of the key ways to understand the market for financial services.

Despite its fundamental importance to strategy-making, segmentation can be difficult and many organisations get it wrong. For example, Volkswagen was the undisputed early leader in the Chinese auto market: in the mid 1990s it had a 50% market share. Its management segmented the market according to products – designing their strategy around choices about which type of vehicles to sell. But this segmentation failed to take account of the major changes in the market during the late 1990s. Early on its main customers were state-owned enterprises, who could be marketed to through the contacts held by Volkswagen's joint venture partner, Shanghai Automobile Industry Corporation. However, as China's economy exploded, retail customers became a more important part of the market. To access these customers required a completely different marketing approach and sales and service network. Segmenting the market by product rather than customer, Volkswagen missed this change, allowing its rivals to build stronger positions.

Note that industry segmentation is not the same as 'customer segmentation', a market research technique that seeks to identify groupings of customers who share common purchasing criteria. Industry segmentation is about dividing up industries according to attractiveness and what it takes to win. For example, when buying cars, young men and young women may belong to different customer segments, with different purchasing criteria, but they are not regarded as separate industry segments because they are not distinctive enough in terms of the rules of the game, growth or profitability.

Another related concept is that of the 'strategic group'. This is a sub-group of competitors in an industry who compete with each other. For example, within the restaurant industry McDonald's competes with Burger King in one strategic group, while local fine dining establishments compete in another. The difference between the concepts of segmentation and groups is that the latter assumes that the company operates in only one business, whereas the concept of segmentation is more flexible. For example, McDonald's competes in two different segments with its burger restaurants and its McCafé coffee shops. This makes it tricky to decide which group it competes in.

HOW TO SEGMENT

Segmentation is often tricky in practice. For example, on what dimensions should you segment the automotive industry? By product (e.g. luxury vs. small cars), by customer type (e.g. fleet sales vs. sales via dealers), by country (e.g. US vs. China), or by type of service (e.g. new car sales vs. servicing). How finely should you segment? For example, should you segment customer types by fleet vs. dealers, or should you sub-divide fleet customers into further segments based on the number of cars purchased, or the typical purchasing behaviour?

In theory, you can segment most businesses into hundreds or thousands of units. There is even a 'segment of one', where every customer is regarded as a different segment. But segmenting too finely can hide important linkages. Global car firms such as Volkswagen, Ford and Toyota may be in many different segments, but these segments are linked because they often share common manufacturing facilities, R&D or dealer networks.

HOW YOU NEED TO DO IT

Segmentation is partly a creative act but also something that can be learned. To segment an industry it can be helpful to begin with the following process:

1. Find alternative ways to segment the industry. Normally this will be by customer need, type of product/service, or stage of the value chain.
2. Choose a segmentation level which helps you focus on the decision that you need to make.
3. Check that the segmentation is neither too detailed, nor at too high a level.

DEVELOPING ALTERNATIVE SEGMENTATIONS

There are normally three ways to segment an industry: market/customer, product/service and value chain, summed up in the more memorable phrase: 'Who? What? How?' A useful first step when segmenting is to brainstorm alternative ways to segment on these dimensions.

Market segmentations can be in terms of geography (e.g. Asia, China, region, city), customer type (e.g. state-owned enterprise vs. consumer), channel (e.g. dealer vs. direct sales) or customer needs (e.g. commuting vs. family trips).

Alternative market segmentations can be derived from changing the level at which the segmentation is made. For example, 'state-owned enterprise' is a very high level – one that is appropriate for discussing major strategy alternatives with head office. For a more detailed strategy it would be worth segmenting state-owned enterprises further – for example, according to the typical number of vehicles they purchase, or whether they buy on the basis of price or relationships.

Product segmentations can also be done in various ways. In the Chinese automotive market, product segmentation could be by the overall type of vehicle, e.g. commercial van vs. passenger vehicle vs. light truck. They might also be divided by price point. As with customer needs, the segmentation could be kept at this level for a strategic debate about the overall strategy for China but broken down into a finer level of detail for a more detailed discussion of the manufacturing strategy.

Customer and product segmentation are the most common but sometimes it is appropriate to segment by different stages in the industry, often described as the 'value chain'. For example, the automotive industry value chain includes parts manufacture, assembly, sales and service, each of which could be a different segment with different ways to win and levels of profitability. Different levels of value chain segmentation are possible. For example, the parts manufacture segment could be divided by the major components of the vehicle – gear box, engine, body parts, axles – each with its own growth rates and competitors.

Segmenting on these three dimensions can lead to any number of potential segmentations, which is clearly not practical. The next step is to pick the most *useful* segmentation.

PICKING A USEFUL SEGMENTATION

The choice of segmentation should support the strategic decision to be made. (If there is no decision, then there is no strategy or segmentation required!)

For example, assume that you are the head of Volkswagen's Chinese business. You need to make decisions about Volkswagen's strategy over the next three to seven years. This involves major choices about which customer, product and parts of the value chain to focus on. Therefore a high-level segmentation that captures the major choices is probably appropriate, for example:

1. Customer segments: state-owned enterprises and end consumers.
2. Product segments: cars, vans, trucks. For each of these segments, high vs. low price.
3. Value chain segments: parts manufacturing (outsource vs. manufacture in house), assembly (outsource vs. in house), sales (own sales force vs. dealer network).

Assume that the outcome of this high-level strategy process is a decision to focus on selling low-priced cars (from the analysis of the product segmentation) to retail customers (customer segmentation), and to assemble the cars from outsourced parts, selling and servicing them through an independent dealer network (value chain segmentation). The next decision facing the company is which regions to operate in and precisely which customers to target. This requires a new level of segmenting on these two dimensions. For example, each region could be analysed as a segment. End-consumers could be segmented according to their income levels or whether they live in the city/countryside, because it is at this level that you need to make decisions.

HOW YOU NEED TO DO IT

Checking Your Segmentation

If you feel unsure or lack experience in segmentation, check to ensure that the segments that you have created are neither too detailed nor at too high a level. The following questions can help you assess the degree of difference between two segments. This will give you a general sense of whether to treat them as one segment, or split them into two. Do the segments –

1. Have very different growth rates?
2. Vary significantly in the average profitability of all competitors?
3. Have major differences in industry structure? (More on this when we discuss the five forces):
   ▶ Are customers different in the two segments? Do they have very different purchasing criteria – for example, are customers in one segment more focused on price while others are more focused on brand or product design?

▶ Are the suppliers different in the two segments?

▶ Are there different potential substitutes for the products in each segment?

4. Have different 'ways to win' or sources of competitive advantage? For example,

▶ Do they have different competitors?

▶ Is your market share or that of competitors in each segment very different?

▶ Are the assets and capabilities required to compete in each segment very different?

▶ Are the cost structures in the two segments different?

▶ Are there significant barriers preventing a competitor in one segment entering the other?

▶ Is your profitability and market share very variable across the two segments?

For example, there are currently significant variations between different regions of China. Markets are growing at very different rates and it is possible to be strongly positioned in one region while being unsuccessful in another (i.e., they have different sources of competitive advantage).

If the segments you have created do not differ significantly on these dimensions, you might consider consolidating them in order to simplify your strategy. For example, you could start by segmenting by region but then decide instead to divide China into four mega-regions, e.g. South, Shanghai, Beijing and Inland – because differences within these mega regions were not significant enough to warrant a more detailed analysis.

Note: there is a Catch 22 involved in segmentation. You need to segment the market *before* you can truly understand its growth rate, inherent profitability and the way to win – but you must first understand what drives attractiveness and what it takes to win *before* you can come up with a sensible segmentation. For this reason, segmentation is often done iteratively, with a mix of intuition and analysis, trial and error. It is one of the hardest topics to learn and requires plenty of practice.

INDUSTRY ATTRACTIVENESS

One of the fundamental questions in strategy is: 'Where to invest?' An important first step is to evaluate the attractiveness of different segments – defined here as how attractive it would be to be a typical competitor in that industry or segment. It has three components:

1. *Size.* All else being equal, it is preferable to compete in a large segment.
2. *Growth.* High growth businesses are not only on their way to becoming bigger, they tend to be more profitable as there is less fighting over market share.
3. *Average profitability.* Some industries are inherently more profitable than others.

For example, in the automotive business the small car segment is large and growing, but generally highly competitive and characterised by low margins. The market for luxury cars is smaller but profitability is higher.

Normally it is possible to find data on size and historic growth. There are exceptions, particularly in exotic segments such as fuel hoses for military aircraft, or speciality food additives. In such cases it may be necessary to do some modelling of the size and growth of the market, e.g. trying to estimate the number of customers, customer growth rate, and what each customer purchases on an annual basis.

Differences in profitability across selected industries

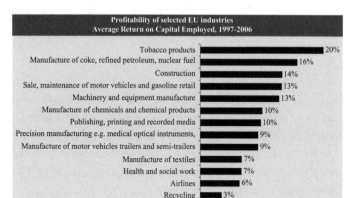

Profitability of selected EU industries
Average Return on Capital Employed, 1997-2006

Industry	%
Tobacco products	20%
Manufacture of coke, refined petroleum, nuclear fuel	16%
Construction	14%
Sale, maintenance of motor vehicles and gasoline retail	13%
Machinery and equipment manufacture	13%
Manufacture of chemicals and chemical products	10%
Publishing, printing and recorded media	10%
Precision manufacturing e.g. medical optical instruments,	9%
Manufacture of motor vehicles trailers and semi-trailers	9%
Manufacture of textiles	7%
Health and social work	7%
Airlines	6%
Recycling	3%

The hardest thing to estimate is often the profitability of a segment. However, as the exhibit shows, there are wide variations in the profitability of different industries, which become more pronounced if industries are segmented more finely.

So it is often necessary to spend some time analysing segment or industry profitability. To do so use a mix of the following approaches:

Identify your own profitability by segment. The advantage of this approach is that the data is usually available. Unfortunately, it won't be a reliable measure of industry segment profitability as it is affected by other factors, such as your competitive position and operating efficiency. Remember, attractiveness is defined as the attractiveness of being a typical participant in the segment. If you are not 'typical' then your profitability will not be an accurate estimate of the average for the segment.

Identify the profitability of a range of competitors. This can be insightful but requires you to find competitors who compete only in one segment, or report data by segment, which is rarely the case. If it is, count yourself lucky. Analysing the profitability of your competitors is a useful benchmark but rarely provides reliable data on which to base major strategic decisions.

Estimate the likely profitability of the segment by considering overall 'industry structure'. Generations of industrial economists have studied what makes some industries more profitable than others. They observe how differences in industry structure (i.e., the mix of suppliers, customers and competitors, and the way they interact) lead to different outcomes for customers and competitors. For example, monopolies lead to high profits for the competitor but a bad deal for customers. Commodity industries, where the product is sold on price, are generally less profitable. Economists have developed some useful rules of thumb that can be used to make an estimate of the likely profitability of an industry segment. So, for example, profitability tends to be lower where there are more competitors in a segment, or when customers are more price-sensitive.The simplest approach is to use a categorisation of types of competitive environment, such as that of Saloner, Shepard and Podolny, from their book

Strategic Management, which characterises types of environment in order of increasing segment profitability:

- ▶ *Perfect competition.* Lots of competitors are selling commodity products to price-sensitive customers. An example would be petrol retailing or farming of commodity products such as wheat.
- ▶ *Niche markets.* Competitors are competing in separate niches, so although there is competition, there aren't too many competitors in any one segment. An example would be luxury goods such as fine wines or high end luggage.
- ▶ *Oligopoly.* There are only a few competitors. These may learn to avoid excessive competition, for example by avoiding attacking each other's core markets, or by not starting price wars. Examples include some electricity generation markets (where there are not many competitors), or UK cinemas (which all show the same films at similar prices)
- ▶ *Dominant firm.* One competitor is strong enough to dictate terms to the industry, such as in pricing and capacity expansion. An example would be retailing of gas and electricity in the UK – British Gas is often the first to announce a price change and regarded as a price benchmark for other competitors.
- ▶ *Monopoly.* There is only one competitor, who can therefore do largely as it wishes – such as

charging high prices. An example would be Microsoft in operating systems.

Industries may not fall into one distinct category. There may be, for example, some competitors in retail electricity who cut prices to gain market share, even if British Gas has not done so. But industries often tend towards a particular model and this will provide a clue as to their profitability. However, it is at best a crude way of estimating likely segment profitability.

THE FIVE FORCES

A more complex but rigorous approach is to use Porter's five forces framework to analyse the profit potential of an industry or segment. According to Porter, five forces determine industry profitability: the threat of substitute products or services, the threat of new entrants, the bargaining power of suppliers, the bargaining power of buyers, and rivalry among existing competitors.

To think about how these forces affect profitability, consider what would happen in an industry were profitability to rise, for example, if all competitors were to put their prices up 20%. In an attractive industry, the extra profits would go to the incumbent competitors because the five forces are favourable (i.e., they all have limited impact). For example, in the tobacco industry:

▶ To a smoker, there is no effective *substitute* for tobacco. There is no risk that a rise in prices will lead to a major switch by customers from tobacco to a substitute product.

▶ There is a low *threat of new entrants* because there are very high barriers to entry – it is expensive to launch and distribute a new tobacco brand. This prevents others from entering the market to take a share of the extra profits.

▶ The most important *suppliers* to the tobacco industry are primarily farmers who have little negotiating power with corporations such as Philip Morris, and are thus unable to get a share of the extra profits.

▶ Similarly, *buyers* of tobacco products are a fragmented bunch with little bargaining power. Since the end user is loyal to one brand, even large retailers cannot credibly threaten to stop buying from a major tobacco firm.

▶ There is limited *industry rivalry* because there are relatively few competitors. Also, they tend not to compete on price because it would not prompt a lot of end users to switch brands. Hence a price war would not benefit anyone.

In contrast, in an industry that is unattractive, the forces would be unfavourable to incumbents. This could result in the increased profits going to the customer, either

WHO YOU NEED TO KNOW
Michael Porter

Michael Porter is the world's most well-known strategy academic. Born in 1947, Porter achieved high academic honours first at Princeton and subsequently at Harvard Business School, where he is currently a professor. He is also co-founder of a management consultancy, Monitor, and an adviser to governments and companies.

One of his great achievements was to be the first to summarise in a digestible format the work of others. He consolidated decades of work by industrial economists such as Ed Mason and Joe Bain, who had studied how differences in the structure of industries – for example the number of competitors, the relative size of customers and competitors, and the existence of barriers to entry – affect profitability. Much of this work was done to understand how to prevent firms asserting monopoly powers and extracting 'unfair' profits. In *Competitive Strategy*, Porter turned this idea on its head to create the five forces framework to help companies understand the conditions under which industry structure could help them enjoy *higher* profits.

His next work, *Competitive Advantage*, articulated and made accessible to a broad audience the concepts of competitive advantage, the difference between competing on cost vs. differentiation, and the value chain. More recently he has applied these ideas to a range of issues, including the competitive advantage of nations and healthcare policy.

Although criticised for not reflecting 'softer' influences on strategy, such as cooperation, culture and government and societal pressures on business, Porter remains the greatest exponent of the economic theories that underpin strategy.

because the incumbents embark on a price war (high rivalry), or because the customer has strong bargaining power, or because there are credible substitutes that the customer can switch to if prices rise. Alternatively, the profits could go to suppliers (if they have strong bargaining power) or to new entrants (if there are low barriers to entry). For example, the European airlines business has low profitability because there is a high level of rivalry (due to overcapacity, a high proportion of fixed costs and price competition), and a credible threat of new entrants (several budget airlines have set up in recent years).

Beyond simply assessing the profit potential of the current industry or segment, Porter's five forces provide a foundation for analysing other aspects of the situation, such as the sources of competitive advantage and insights into how the industry may evolve. For this reason, it is a useful analysis to apply early on when devising strategy in a competitive industry.

To do a five forces analysis, first assess which are likely to have a big impact on industry profitability. The following checklist may be helpful:

The threat of substitute products or services is high when:

▶ substitutes have competitive price and quality;
▶ buyers face few switching costs.

The threat of new entrants is high when there are:

- few economies of scale;
- limited experience or learning curve effects;
- limited product differentiation;
- low capital requirements;
- low switching costs;
- ready access to distribution channels;
- limited advantages for incumbents from other sources, e.g.:
  - proprietary product technology;
  - favourable access to raw materials;
  - favourable locations;
  - government subsidies.

The bargaining power of suppliers is high when:

- there are few suppliers and they are more concentrated than the industry they sell to;
- they are not obliged to compete with other substitute products for sales to the industry;
- the industry is not an important customer of the supplier group;
- the supplier's product is an important input to the buyer's business;
- the supplier group's products are differentiated or have built up switching costs;
- the supplier group poses a credible threat of forward integration.

The bargaining power of buyers is high when:

- ▶ buyers are concentrated or purchase large volumes relative to seller sales;
- ▶ the products buyers purchase represent a significant fraction of their costs or purchases;
- ▶ the products buyers purchase are standard or undifferentiated;
- ▶ buyers face few switching costs;
- ▶ buyers earn low profits;
- ▶ buyers pose a credible threat of backward integration;
- ▶ the industry's product is unimportant to the quality of the buyers' products or services;
- ▶ the buyer has full information.

Rivalry among existing competitors is high when there are:

- ▶ numerous or equally-balanced competitors;
- ▶ slow industry growth;
- ▶ high fixed or storage costs;
- ▶ limited differentiation or switching costs;
- ▶ diverse competitors;
- ▶ high strategic stakes;
- ▶ high exit barriers;
- ▶ capacity is augmented in large increments.

Having assessed these factors, integrate your thinking into a judgement about the effect of the forces on overall industry profitability. It may be helpful to think of the earlier chart which showed the profitability of different industries. Is your industry more like tobacco (highly profitable) or more like the airline industry (highly competitive, low return)?

ISSUES WITH USING THE FIVE FORCES FRAMEWORK

Porter's five forces framework is an extremely useful tool for understanding the factors driving the profit potential of an industry. However, one source of frustration is that it does not provide a quantitative answer; ultimately a judgment is required. Of course, you can and should check that whatever data you have about profitability is consistent with the five forces analysis, but it's not the same as being able to precisely model industry profitability. Numerous attempts have been made to come up with a tool that does this, but they have largely failed.

There are some exceptions. In commodity businesses such as minerals or electricity generation, for example, it is possible to draw supply/demand curves to estimate the likely price and thus the profitability of an industry. It may be that your particular industry is amenable to such an analysis, or an alternative quantitative analysis. Even if no firm predictions can be made, such models can provide support to or challenge more qualitative approaches, such as the five forces.

Various other issues can trip people up when estimating industry and segment profitability. The first is that they are not clear about what is meant by 'segment profitability'. They often confuse this with 'our profitability in this segment', assuming, for example, that highly profitable products must be in attractive segments – when you may be profitable because you have a very strong competitive position albeit in an unattractive segment. As mentioned, Porter's five forces gives an insight into the potential profitability of a general participant in the segment – not that of a specific competitor. The important point to remember is that the overall profit potential, size and growth of a segment is independent of your own position in that segment.

Another issue is that the concept of 'industry attractiveness' works best when the different players face a similar industry structure. For example, all major car companies have a common customer base, common suppliers of raw materials such as steel, and common barriers to entry. When there are few competitors, or these competitors face very different industry structures, then each may exist in a 'micro climate' where the industry structure is unique. For example, some airlines have strong unions (suppliers of labour), others do not, so the five forces analysis cannot simplistically be applied at the industry level. If there is no 'typical' competitor, an analysis of the industry can be difficult. Fortunately, the five forces can still be used to evaluate the likely profitability of a company's individual position, but it will have to be tweaked to assess the individual situation of each company, making the application of the framework more complex. Nevertheless, the insights derived from the forces shaping profitability will still be valid.

A particular limitation is that, unlike many of the strategy concepts and tools discussed in this book, the concept of industry profitability is not easily transferable or relevant to all not-for-profit organisations. The concept of 'industry profitability' is not easily applicable to a charity (unless it is competing in an industry such as with charity shops). However, the more general concept of 'attractiveness' remains relevant. For example, if you are a charity that is dedicated to improving the lives of poor children, there are many 'segments' you could operate in – different countries and different services, such as water supply, education, food programmes, career development, etc. Each can be evaluated in terms of attractiveness by considering the degree to which operating in those segments would contribute to improving the lives of poor children (the equivalent of 'potential profitability' for a profit seeking entity). Would a pound spent on education have more impact than a pound spent on water supply? The basic notion of 'attractiveness' remains relevant for a charity, even if it is defined in a different way.

THE MACRO-ENVIRONMENT

In many industries, the role of external factors beyond rivals, new entrants, suppliers and buyers can have an important influence on strategy. For example, government regulations, public opinion and pressure groups can be influential.

Some argue that such influences, referred to by Porter as the 'macro-environment', can best be evaluated by thinking of how they affect market forces or 'micro-environment'. Consider the influence of governments on the airline industry, for example. Laws that restrict foreign companies operating in and out of a country raise barriers to entry and reduce the number of rivals. The regulation of airports limits the ability of these potentially powerful suppliers to negotiate profits from the airlines. For example, the owner of Heathrow airport could earn a fortune by auctioning slots but is prevented from doing so by regulation.

But the macro environment does not always operate through the market forces of the micro-environment. For example, volcanic ash clouds from Iceland affected the entire airline industry – but not through any of the five forces. Public anger in the US over the BP oil spill in the Gulf of Mexico similarly had a major effect, but not through the marketplace.

For such influences it can be helpful to use a different framework to evaluate the effect of broader forces on the organisation. The most common form of analysis is PEST or PESTLE analysis, which stands for:

▶ **P**olitical,
▶ **E**conomic
▶ **S**ocial
▶ **T**echnological
▶ **L**egal and
▶ **E**nvironmental influences

This simple structure will help you to collect information on these various environmental forces; the key then is to derive their implications for the organisation. This can be done in two complementary ways. The first is to think about how they impact the five forces. The second is to ask if they will have any other effects that could occur not through the process of competition but by some other mechanism, e.g. government fiat, the force of public opinion, or an act of God.

Frameworks similar to PESTLE analysis can be useful. A common one is 'country risk analysis', which seeks to describe the general factors at play in a particular country. This can be particularly helpful if you are considering a major overseas investment. In effect, it is a type of PESTLE analysis customised to the issues typically encountered when making investments in unfamiliar or risky markets. These might include:

▶ economic uncertainties (e.g. growth, inflation);
▶ sovereign risk (risk that the government might default on its debt and other agreements);
▶ political uncertainties;

▶ foreign exchange transfer restrictions, including restrictions on dividend repatriation;

▶ exchange rate volatility including the risk of a revaluation;

▶ taxation policies and risk of retroactive action;

▶ regulatory and legal uncertainties;

▶ risks of conflict (civil war or other types of unrest);

▶ level of corruption.

As with PESTLE analysis, think through how these factors will influence the industry's growth rate and profitability.

Country analysis is often customised to the context. For example, if you are investing in a power plant in a developing country, factors such as the legal enforceability of fuel supply contracts and the reliability of the electricity transmission structure will be particularly important. The aim is to come up with a customised approach rather than to simply consult standard credit risk reports (which tend to be about specific issues such as the creditworthiness of government debt).

WHAT YOU NEED TO READ

▶ For a worked example of how to apply the tools in this chapter (and subsequent chapters), see *www.whatyouneedtoknowaboutstrategy.com*.

▶ One of the few practical guides to segmentation is Chapter 2 of Richard Koch's book, *The Financial Times Guide to Strategy*, Pearson, 2006 (also on Google Books).

▶ The original five forces framework was published in *Competitive Strategy* by Michael Porter, Free Press, 1980. An update can be found in 'The Five Competitive Forces That Shape Strategy' in the *Harvard Business Review*, January 2008.

▶ Robert Grant's *Contemporary Strategy Analysis*, John Wiley & Sons Ltd, 2010 has two chapters in part two discussing Industry analysis.

▶ Consolidated views of free online information are available through Companies House and the British Library. It is also possible to access paid databases of industry and economic trends (e.g. Oxford Analytica, Strategy Eye) as well as specialist research databases (e.g. Nexis Lexis, Infotrac) and analyst sites such as (in the IT sector) Gartner and Forrester.

▶ Specialist portals provide a single point of entry to appropriate sources of information on specific topics, such as EBSCO's EDS and British Library's Resource Navigator that help to access resources on strategy, the Ashridge Virtual Learning Resource Centre for management development and leadership, and the DTN 'scenario console' for a unique snapshot of current trends.

IF YOU ONLY REMEMBER ONE THING

Before you start to analyse your own organisation, step back and look at the external environment.

CHAPTER 3

FROM THE INSIDE

WHAT IT'S ALL ABOUT

- ▶ Generating value for customers
- ▶ Assessing competitive advantage
- ▶ Defining the mission and objectives
- ▶ Summarising the overall situation
- ▶ Cross-checking with actual performance

Multiple aspects of the internal situation can be evaluated – for example, products, services, brand, costs, technology, people, skills, systems, organisation structure and culture, leadership, vision, performance, and financial strength. So where do you start?

To focus your thinking and data collection, consider that the only things that matter about the inside are those that affect the fit of the organisation with its environment. Products, services and brand have to be understood in the context of how they deliver value for customers. Costs and technology need to be evaluated not in absolute terms, but how they compare to competitors.

Bearing in mind this need to focus on how the internals fit with environment, there are just a few important questions that need to be answered. The first is: *How much value are we creating for customers and stakeholders?* To avoid a navel-gazing exercise about your own organisation, ask yourself what it is that you do to meet the needs of those you serve. What value do you create for them? What makes them want to buy, or not buy, your product or service? This is sometimes described as a CVP (customer value proposition) or USP (unique selling point). It can also be used to describe the perspective of other important stakeholders, e.g. employees, partners, government, donors and local communities.

The second question is: *What is your competitive advantage?* Or, to be blunt, *Are you winning?* In a competitive market, being good at serving customers is not enough. You have to be better than the competition.

It may seem surprising to start an analysis of the 'internal' situation by involving customers, stakeholders and competitors, but internal capabilities and characteristics are only valuable if they create more value for stakeholders than competitors. By focusing on these two questions you will be less likely to fall into the trap of listing what your organisation is good at, rather than seeing how those characteristics contribute to its success or failure.

One other important aspect of the internal situation is: *What are our current mission and objectives?* While your performance may ultimately be determined by your competitive position, you need to understand what your organisation is ultimately trying to achieve – your mission and strategic objectives.

CREATING VALUE FOR CUSTOMERS

Why start with customers? Because being the strongest competitor is not very rewarding if you do not create any value for customers – as the leading producers of horse-drawn carriages, vacuum tubes, and vinyl records will testify.

Those who find new ways of creating value for customers often end up as market leaders. Apple created the iPod and the iPhone, Google its search engine, McDonald's provides reliable fast food at low cost, Fairtrade enables consumers to support developing country producers, Oxfam ensures that your donations are put to good use, and so on. All of these organisations were leaders in creating new sources of value for their customers and stakeholders.

WHO SAID IT . . .

"Profit in business comes from repeat customers, customers that boast about your product and service, and that bring friends with them."
– W. Edwards Deming

Finding new ways to create value through what is some-times termed *value innovation*, is particularly helpful for new businesses. It also appeals to the hopes of many managers in mature organisations who know how tough it is to operate in mature, competitive markets.

Note that some organisations have more than one customer. For example, traditional newspapers or magazines compete for both readers and advertisers. In such businesses each customer needs to be analysed separately.

The analysis can also be performed for 'stakeholders' rather than 'customers'.

EVALUATING CUSTOMER VALUE CREATION

There are many ways to collect information about what your customers value and how they view your organisation, including talking to sales people, analysing competitor products, conducting customer, distributor or retailer interviews, carrying out focus groups or market research, and comparing prices and market shares of different products.

What you need is a simple tool to draw together the implications of the data collected. A simple first step is to list customers' purchasing criteria. For example, the following factors might influence how a tourist travelling from London to a holiday destination selects a particular airline:

- ▶ price;
- ▶ ambience of the airport;
- ▶ convenience of airport location;
- ▶ comfort of the seat;
- ▶ convenience of flight time;
- ▶ reliability;
- ▶ friendliness of staff;
- ▶ perks for frequent traveller.

Having identified the basis on which customers make their choices you can now compare your 'customer value proposition' (CVP) vs. that of competitors. A useful tool to use is a 'value curve'. For example, a comparison between BA and Ryanair on the purchasing criteria listed above might look like the following:

Value curve for two airlines

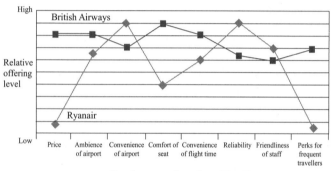

Key elements or dimensions of the offer
Adapted for Blue Ocean Strategy, Kim and Mauborgne 1999

This tool provides a simple way of comparing CVPs and works particularly well for mass market products. It also helps in sparking and focusing a debate – for example, you might disagree with the chart and have a different view on Ryanair and BA. Initial discussions should be followed by more detailed customer research.

Note that the value curve describes the product but says little about how customers weigh the importance of each of the criteria. A useful refinement is to circle the most important criteria, or rank them.

THE IMPORTANCE OF COMPETITIVE ADVANTAGE

Creating value is vital but not sufficient. As stated earlier, in a competitive market you have to do so *better* than alternative providers. For example, traditional airlines undoubtedly created a lot of value for customers, as demonstrated by the steady growth of the industry, but low-cost airlines created even more value, and have grown much faster than their traditional counterparts. Similarly, Nokia undoubtedly made great mobile phones, but Apple's iPhone was better, and was therefore able to win significant market share. It is not the value you create that counts, but the extent to which you create *more* value than competitors.

A fundamental idea in business strategy is that competitive advantage is the key to long-term success. In a competitive marketplace, the organisation which has an advantage should enjoy a virtuous circle of winning more customers, achieving economies of scale, making higher margins, investing in better products, and thus winning yet more customers.

As evidence of the importance of competitive advantage, consider that profits in most businesses are highest for the leading competitor. According to one study, the leading competitor in the average industry made a return on investment of 32%, while the number two made only 22% – being the best was worth a full 10 percentage points of profitability. Some businesses can be described as 'winner takes all' – there is only one successful competitor. ('Network' businesses such as eBay, Google or Facebook tend to have these characteristics). In other industries, coming second or third provides a reasonable living but the goal is still to be as close to the number one competitor as possible.

A strong competitive position can outweigh the disadvantages of being in a tough industry. Ryanair, for example, is profitable in the notoriously tough airlines business. A competitive advantage can even compensate for being mediocre at operations. For example, Saudi Arabia does not claim to have the best technology for extracting oil, or to have unique skills in operating oil fields, but it enjoys a competitive advantage in oil production because its costs of extraction are so low.

Competitive advantage is such a vital concept that there is a vast debate about its roots. To be a good strategist you need to understand something of this debate, the sources of advantage in your business, and how competitive your organisation is.

DIFFERENT WAYS TO EVALUATE ADVANTAGE

A simple way of thinking about advantage is that it comes in two forms – *cost* and *customer value* or *differentiation*. In other words, something is an advantage only if it allows organisations to have lower costs or to provide higher value to customers. It is hard to be both a cost and differentiation leader, as such companies risk being 'caught in the middle'. However, there are a few, exceptional organisations who compete successfully on a mix of both dimensions – for example, Singapore Airlines and Toyota.

Another way of thinking about advantage is that it comes from the *positions* that an organisation owns. A position

WHO YOU NEED TO KNOW
Bruce Henderson

Henderson (1915–1992), founder of the Boston Consulting Group (BCG), was one of the most innovative thinkers about strategy. Like Michael Porter and Henry Mintzberg, Henderson studied engineering and, like Porter, attended Harvard Business School, leaving early to work for Westinghouse. He was named one of Time Magazine's top 10 news-makers under 30 years old.

Henderson set up a consulting arm for the Boston Safe Deposit and Trust Company in 1963, spinning it off as BCG in 1974. Henderson developed and popularised many important concepts, including the Experience Curve (stating that costs come down in relation to the cumulative production of the product) and the famous Growth-Share Matrix (with its 'cash cows', 'stars', 'dogs', and 'question marks'). He drew attention to competitive advantage as the driver of long-term success. His timing was perfect as US companies, grown fat on the post-war boom, suddenly needed to reassess their corporate strategies following the oil crisis of 1973 and the emergence of Japanese competitors.

A brilliant man who was also a great communicator, his pithy 'perspectives', consisting of a few hundred words which delivered a powerful insight, were read widely. Under Henderson BCG was an innovative, creative organisation, although it suffered, as Henderson did, from a lack of focus on serving its customers' needs, being more inclined towards intellectual elegance.

A number of other insightful strategists developed at BCG under Henderson's leadership and influence, such as Tom Hout, Philip Evans, Tom Wurster and George Stalk. Others, such as Bill Bain, left to form their own companies. BCG also inspired competitors, such as McKinsey, to develop their own strategy practices.

provides the ability to earn a superior return, such as a brand, patent, market share, or privileged access to low-cost resources. Valuable positions are typically difficult to develop – particularly in a mature business – although they can often be bought and sold. In the 1960s and 70s, companies with strong positions appeared to be the most successful in the long run, whether they were in mature markets such as cars (GM and Ford) or earth moving equipment (Caterpillar), or higher growth markets such as computers (IBM) or photocopiers (Xerox).

However, as the 1980s and 90s demonstrated, even companies with strong positions could be outmanoeuvred. Toyota and Honda took on the US auto giants, and Komatsu caught up with Caterpillar. Emerging competitors such as Compaq, Intel and Microsoft took market share away from IBM, as did Canon from Xerox.

Part of the reason for the success of these competitors, who started out at a positional disadvantage, was their emphasis on building and using the superior *capabilities* that resulted from combining an aspirational organisational culture with new technology and manufacturing processes. These allowed them to be more efficient and provide superior products, out-competing larger but more cumbersome and less capable competitors. (There is an arcane argument about the differences between 'capabilities' and 'competencies' that is not reviewed here – so consider them as equivalent).

WHO SAID IT . . .

". . . the essence of strategy is not the structure of a company's position in products and markets, but the dynamics of its behaviours."
– **George Stalk**

For example, Honda used its leaner manufacturing processes and expertise in the internal combustion engine to sell cheaper and more reliable cars. Canon used its expertise in lenses to build market share in photocopiers.

WHO YOU NEED TO KNOW
Tom Peters

Tom Peters is one of the most provocative thinkers and speakers on strategy. Born in 1942, he studied engineering at Cornell and completed an MBA and PhD at Stanford. Peters served in Vietnam and was a senior White House advisor on drug abuse before joining management consultants McKinsey in 1974. He quickly became involved in a project to identify what made organisations effective. He and his colleagues soon realised that the answer went beyond structure and strategy – McKinsey's view at the time.

Working with Robert Waterman, Peters put together a view on excellence that turned into the best-selling book *In Search of*

Excellence. Ultimately, the pair would prove the accuracy of the adage that 'no prophet is welcome in his hometown' – both leaving McKinsey to work independently.

'*In Search of Excellence*' argued that the key to strategic sense was operational and organisational excellence, as well as what others later termed 'capabilities' – captured in eight themes including 'bias for action', 'close to the customer', 'simple and lean organisational structures', and 'stick to the knitting'. Inspirational for some, others thought it deeply flawed, especially when a third of the 'excellent' companies profiled in the book were in serious financial and strategic difficulties within a few years. It also introduced the famous 7S framework – derided by some for its lack of rigour and lauded by others as a counterbalance to the narrow-mindedness of economists as exemplified by Michael Porter.

Peters is an inspirational speaker. He laid the ground for similar gurus such as Richard

Pascale, Rosabeth Moss Kanter, John Kotter, Jim Collins and Gary Hamel. He provides a reminder that strategy is only as valuable as the quality of its execution. One of his favourite quotes is 'Execution is strategy'. However, he and his followers failed to create strong intellectual underpinnings, unlike Porter's economics-based view of strategy. Peters sparked a revolution, but it is still just that – an anti–establishment challenge, but not a well-researched and consistent replacement.

Particular attention has focused recently on those capabilities that allow organisations to respond effectively to turbulent change. Don Sull, a professor at London Business School, has highlighted how *adaptability* and *resilience* are of particular value as sources of advantage at such times. A strategic dilemma for many organisations is how to manage the compromise between the benefits of being highly focused on optimising their current competitive position, while retaining enough excess resources to survive lean times and adapt to changing situations.

The implication is that it can be helpful to look at competitive advantage in two ways: How well suited is an organisation to its current environment? And how able is it to adapt and survive turbulent change?

WHO SAID IT ...

"You have to be fast on your feet and adaptive, or else a strategy is useless."
– Charles de Gaulle

A competitive advantage is more valuable if it is *sustainable* – in other words, it is not easily copied. For example, the production facilities of the clothes retailer Zara allow it to customise the colours and designs of the items in its stores. This is a relatively sustainable source of advantage because it is difficult to copy, unlike a retail strategy based on extending opening hours or having a sale, which can be rapidly copied by competitors.

The following figure shows how different ways of thinking about advantage fit together. The roots of competitive advantage are the capabilities of an organisation, which gives rise to its positions. These are of value if they bear the two fruits of advantage – lower costs or higher value. The more sustainable these advantages are, the better. A further source of advantage is the breadth of the tree – the ability to avoid being over-reliant on a narrow niche. This can be achieved by being agile or by having abundant resources, such as a strong balance sheet or a global scope that foster resilience in times of trouble.

The key idea to take away from this section is that competitive advantage comes from a broad network of

Different perspectives on competitive advantage

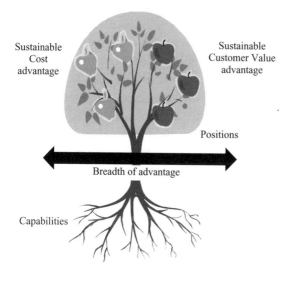

Sustainable Cost advantage

Sustainable Customer Value advantage

Positions

Breadth of advantage

Capabilities

positions and capabilities that lead to sustainably low costs and high levels of customer value. Understanding exactly how this network operates can be difficult, requiring a mix of analysing hard data, such as costs and prices, and soft data, such as the motivation of the staff and management team. It also requires a broad range of data covering the organisation, its competitors and the environment. Fortunately, there are many tips, tools and frameworks that can help. A selection is presented below, with further references at the end of the chapter.

EVALUATING COST AND CUSTOMER VALUE ADVANTAGE

A very direct approach to evaluating your competitive advantage is to compare your costs and price point with those of different competitors, although this normally requires extensive data collection, modelling and some educated guesses. The exhibit below offers a comparison of the cost and average price per passenger mile for a traditional and a low-cost airline. The stacked bars represent the major elements of cost for each competitor. The lines at the top of the bars indicate the price.

The reasons for differences between the two types of competitor are summarised on the right of the chart. For example, budget airlines typically have 20% more seats and enjoy a 30% higher utilisation of those seats –

Example: Advantage of low cost airlines

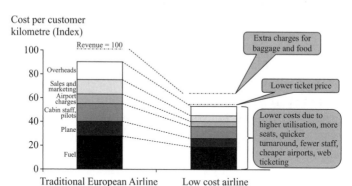

Cost per customer
kilometre (Index)

Revenue = 100

Extra charges for
baggage and food

Lower ticket price

Lower costs due to
higher utilisation, more
seats, quicker
turnaround, fewer staff,
cheaper airports, web
ticketing

100 ─

80 ─   Overheads

60 ─   Sales and
          marketing
          Airport
          charges
          Cabin staff,
          pilots
40 ─
          Plane
20 ─
          Fuel
0 ─

Traditional European Airline   Low cost airline

providing significant cost savings on fuel, plane leasing, staff and airport charges.

This approach forces the strategist to be precise about the size, nature and drivers of advantage. However, it can be difficult to obtain the data required, so personal judgment and some back-of-the-envelope calculations will be required.

To make this approach work, it is best to start with your own cost structure and average prices and think through how these might vary for your competitors. For example, in the exhibit above, the starting information was the cost structure of a traditional airline. Differences in average prices were estimated using travel websites. Data on the number of seats and utilisation of planes were collected through surveys of budget airlines carried out in airports.

EVALUATING POSITIONAL SOURCES OF ADVANTAGE

Cost and customer value advantages are partly generated by the positions of an organisation, such as market share, customer relationships, long-term contracts or established distribution networks. However, positional advantage is a rather woolly concept. The following checklist will help you make an assessment:

▶ *Market positions arising from the benefits of market share, scale, experience and scope.* Market share often provides a competitive advantage. For example, GE enjoys a scale advantage in its gas turbine business because, as market leader, it is able to spread its R&D costs over a bigger base of business. It also benefits from 'experience curve' effects, whereby the more gas turbines it makes, the more the cost of production declines due to the learning acquired. Because it makes more turbines than anyone else, GE has the greatest experience curve effects, the lowest costs, and the most advanced products. 'Scope' effects are the benefits of competing across a range of segments. For example, GE's presence in financial services enables its turbine business to provide attractive financing packages to potential customers.

▶ *Brand and reputation.* A strong brand can be a particularly valuable source of advantage, particularly in consumer goods. Brands may be closely linked to scale advantage, as in the case of Ford or Coca Cola, for example, but advantages can also come from having a distinct position in a market or niche, such as Red Bull or Bollinger champagne.

▶ *Value chain design and vertical integration.* Having particular positions along the industry value chain (i.e., the sequence of activities involved in the industry) can bestow an advantage. For example, the personal computer industry value chain includes activities such as the manufacture of hardware, software, marketing, retailing and after-sales service. Apple has chosen to remain relatively vertically integrated – having a presence in all of these activities – in contrast to many of its competitors. This is currently a source of advantage, allowing Apple to have a distinct positioning in laptop computers, although at times the extra costs of this strategy have nearly sunk the company.

▶ *Access to unique resources or relationships.* Pharmaceutical companies extract huge value from the patents they hold. Mining companies seek to secure the lowest cost sources of minerals. National defence companies typically gain a significant share of national defence spending due to their political influence. All these illustrate the advantages that flow from favoured access to intellectual property, raw materials, technology, suppliers, customers or government relationships.

▶ *Input costs.* In mature, low-tech industries such as textiles, clothing or plastic toys, access to low-cost labour can be key. Other inputs may be important, such as low-cost energy. Large aluminium plants, which use a lot of electricity, are often located near a source of low-cost hydro power.

▶ *Focus.* Being a specialist can provide an advantage, often through a mix of the sources described above. German mid-sized companies are often highly specialised (for example, in garden rose breeding, glockenspiels, portable sanitation or ring tones). Being a specialist provides a range of positional advantages such as scale within a niche, experience, brand, vertical integration and access to specialist local suppliers.

EVALUATING CAPABILITIES

As with sources of positional advantage, it can be helpful to have a checklist of different types of capability which create advantage. Such lists can be grouped either in terms of the benefits of the capabilities (e.g. speed, operational effectiveness, agility and innovativeness), or the nature of the capabilities themselves. Examples of the latter include:

▶ *IT and logistics systems.* The success of both Wal-Mart and Tesco is based on the ability of their logistics systems not only to stock the shelves, but to provide actionable information to management about what is selling.

▶ *Processes.* Cisco has developed standardised processes for acquiring and integrating new technology companies, allowing it to remain at the forefront of the rapidly developing hardware businesses in which it competes.

▶ *Skills.* Many Italian mid-sized companies and the regions in which they are located seek to be the most skilled in particular niches, such as glass manufacturing in Murano.

▶ *People.* Consulting companies such as McKinsey and BCG pride themselves on their ability to attract the best and the brightest. BCG uses a particular metric to measure success in recruiting: the percentage of candidates who have had an offer from both McKinsey and BCG, but who eventually choose BCG. Small companies often rely on one or two exceptional key people.

▶ *Organisational structure.* Companies often reorganise to generate more value from their businesses. For example, Unilever took some of the decision-making powers from its highly autonomous country organisations and put it in the hands of global product managers.

▶ *Organisational culture, style, values and behavioural norms.* Southwest Airlines developed a culture based on having fun (as well as working hard) that differentiated it from the more fractious workforces of its traditional rivals.

Another way to map capabilities is the 7S model, which can be investigated further via a web search.

Note that the distinction between positional and capability advantages is not always clear. Don't worry about which category a particular source of advantage belongs to; the distinction is intended only to ensure that you generate a comprehensive list of what drives advantage in the industry.

ARE WE WINNING?

With so many ways to evaluate value creation and competitive advantage, it is easy to end up with a lot of lists and a mishmash of ideas. A relatively simple method for drawing this thinking together is shown in the following chart, which provides an overall perspective on how well your organisation is doing. It collates all the analysis covered in this chapter into a view of how well you are serving customers and how well you rank against your competitors, as a basis for debate about any further improvements that could be made.

The top box on the left shows the market segment being evaluated (don't forget that competition occurs primarily at the segment level). The example compares a potential budget competitor to British Airways and Virgin on the highly profitable London/New York route. The box in the top right adds the customer perspective,

Comparison of competitive advantage

Example for a budget airline competing on London/New York Route

Target market segment: Business traveller from London to New York	Product characteristics that drive customer value: Price, Convenience of departure time, Location of the terminal, Comfort of seat, Reliability, Connections, Friendliness of staff, Food and drink quality

Sources of advantage	% Weight now	% Weight 2015	Budget Airline	BA	Virgin	Management effort	Financial resources
Market share on NY-London route	20	20	1	5	3	●●	●●●
Market share of forwarding connections	20	15	1	5	3	●●	●●●
Perks for frequent travellers	20	20	4	4	3	●	
Comfortable service	30	35	2	5	5		
Low cost structure	10	10	5	2	3	●●	
		TOTAL*	2.6	4.2	3.4		

* Total should be weighted – for simplicity, not shown here

Note: Developed from an original by David Stadler

highlighting the dimensions on which a customer will evaluate competitors' offerings. This makes it easier to check back that the sources of advantage will deliver what customers value in terms of price and value.

The main table defines the primary sources of advantage, which are a mix of positions (e.g. market share), customer value (perks for frequent travellers) and capabilities (motivated staff, lean overhead structure). Deciding which are the key sources of advantage involves first going through the analyses described earlier and then making a judgment call about which are most important.

This should prompt questions about how the sources of advantage might change (in this case, the business is seen as stable), how different competitors rank today (the budget airline is disadvantaged on several important dimensions), and the implications for the airline's management team and investment programme. The table format provides a great one-pager for discussion and links analysis to action. Variants on this simple approach are easy to generate.

(A cautionary note: If some competitors have a very different business model, this approach may underestimate their strength because it rates all competitors on the same sources of advantage. For example, if we were to use the same table to evaluate competition on the London/Paris route, it could be difficult to define the sources of advantage for Eurostar or self-drive using a ferry, both of which are significant competitors.)

THE VALUE CHAIN

The competitive advantage matrix is only one of many approaches to exploring how value and advantage are created. As this is such a crucial issue for strategists, it is worth having a few other approaches in your toolkit.

One that has already been described is to draw up the *cost and revenue structures* of different competitors, such as for the budget airlines mentioned above. This can yield a similar discussion and insights to that generated by the competitive advantage matrix, although with less focus on what the management actions should be.

A similar approach is to use the *value chain* – one of the most popular tools in use today, first popularised by Michael Porter. The value chain is the sequence of activities that an organisation executes, e.g. R&D, product design, production, marketing & sales, distribution and customer service (the actual sequence will vary according to the industry). Value chain analysis starts by describing the value chain for a particular organisation and uses this as the basis for a series of further analyses. One such analysis is to ask which parts of the value chain create value for customers. For example, a lot of value is created by Apple in product design, whereas Cristal Champagne, which retails at £150 per bottle, creates value through its marketing.

Another analysis is to determine which parts of the value chain are sources of advantage or disadvantage for a particular organisation. Apple has significant competitive advantage in purchasing (due to its scale), product design (due to its scale and experienced staff) and brand image, for example. However, it has no advantage in after-sales service; indeed it may even have higher costs than some competitors.

DEFINING THE MISSION AND OBJECTIVES

Another important aspect of the internal situation is the current objective, as future strategy options should be consistent with that objective. It is important to distinguish between an organisation's strategic objective and its mission – both of which are important to understand. The *strategic objective*, e.g. 'enter a new market', 'defend market share', or 'increase profit by 25%', is typically subsidiary to the overall *mission* of the organisation, e.g. 'to refresh the world' (from Coca Cola's mission statement).

The mission can be tricky to identify. What is written in the formal mission statement – if indeed one exists – is often not what is perceived by, and motivates, the individuals in the organisation. It can therefore be useful to have some tools for understanding the overall mission of an organisation. Two such tools are the Ashridge Mission Diamond and Stakeholder Analysis.

In their book, *A Sense of Mission*, Andrew Campbell and Sally Yeung posit that an organisation's mission is captured not by what is written in the mission statement, but by what is really believed and acted upon. This 'sense of mission' can be captured by examining four components – purpose, strategy, values, and standards and behaviours (see figure below).

As an example, consider the YHA (Youth Hostel Association), a charity which owns and operates a chain of hostels around the UK. The historic *purpose* of the YHA was to 'Help all, especially young people of limited means, to a greater knowledge, love and care of the countryside.' The *strategy* to achieve this was to build a network of volunteer-run rural hostels, which made them

The Ashridge Mission Diamond

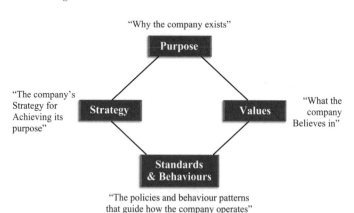

cheap and provided access to the countryside for young people. The *values* were to be open to all, particularly to young people. The *behaviours* were those of a volunteer-run organisation – those in charge hostels were given significant autonomy to run the hostels as they saw fit, while guests were required to do chores to keep costs to a minimum.

Note that the strategic objective is only one of the four elements of the mission – illustrating its critical but subsidiary role.

The Ashridge Diamond is a useful tool for describing the overall mission of the organisation and the strategic objective. It also provides an initial evaluation of the overall sense of mission and any conflicts there may be with the current strategy. To be powerful, there has to be a good fit between the various corners of the Diamond.

In the case of the historic YHA there was a good fit. However, in recent years, the strategy has been changed to reflect the changing needs of the tourist market. Small, primarily rural hostels have been sold off and the cash invested in building hostels in more popular, urban locations. Visitors are no longer required to do chores and there has been an attempt to professionalise the management of hostels. As a result there has been some conflict between the strategy and other points of the Diamond. The management of the YHA has restated the purpose: 'To help all, especially young people of limited means, to a greater knowledge, love and care of the countryside, **and appreciation of the cultural values of towns and cities**.' Nevertheless, the changes have been controversial within the organisation.

STAKEHOLDER ANALYSIS

In addition to an organisation's mission, it can be useful to understand the broader context within which the mission is set, particularly if there are many influential stakeholders. Stakeholders rarely define the mission – that is something that is typically done within the organisation – but they do put constraints on what that mission can be.

Imagine, for example, that you are part of a local council that has to establish a mission that reconciles pressures from the voting public, local businesses and organisations, customers of council services, employees, suppliers, central and regional government organisations, national politicians, special interest groups, and local political party organisations. To conduct a stakeholder analysis, evaluate each one's motivations, interests, requirements and the extent of their power and influence. From this, draw conclusions about the constraints within which the mission of the organisation is pursued. The results may be messy, but that is the point. Conflicting pressures need to be mapped out and understood as part of the assessment of the current situation.

SUMMARISING THE OVERALL SITUATION

The external and internal assessments described in these last two chapters should provide a great deal of information. How can you bring all the thinking together into a concise statement about the situation?

The most common tool used is a SWOT analysis. The idea is to document the strengths, weaknesses, opportunities and threats, and then come up with a strategy that seizes the opportunities and counteracts the threats by addressing weaknesses and building on strengths. There are two problems with SWOT analysis. The first is that a strength can also be a weakness, and an opportunity can be a threat. For example, the low inventories required by Japanese companies are typically seen as a strength because they lower costs and increase flexibility. However in China they were a weakness because of the unreliable nature of suppliers, and thus the higher risk of a disruption in deliveries. Similarly, global warming may represent an opportunity for wind turbine manufacturers in the West, but a threat for farmers in the low-lying deltas of Bangladesh. SWOT analysis can fool organisations into serious misjudgements about their position. A second problem is that SWOT does not include any reference to the goals of the organisation.

A superior variant of SWOT – although less well known – is the Strategy Triangle, shown in the following diagram. To use it, first list an organisation's objectives, internal capabilities (broadly defined to include positions) and external opportunities at the three points of the triangle. At this stage there need be no judgement about whether the capabilities are a strength or a weakness, or whether the opportunities are attractive or threatening.

Next, ask whether there is a good fit between these three. For example, do the capabilities provide the necessary strengths required to address each of the opportunities? Do the opportunities offer the potential for the objectives to be achieved?

Consider, as an example, a small high-tech business with a new type of voice-recognition software, spun off from a university and run by three academics who have set themselves the strategic objective of developing a

The Strategy Triangle

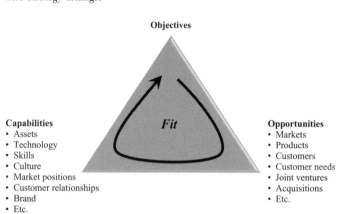

Objectives

Fit

Capabilities
• Assets
• Technology
• Skills
• Culture
• Market positions
• Customer relationships
• Brand
• Etc.

Opportunities
• Markets
• Products
• Customers
• Customer needs
• Joint ventures
• Acquisitions
• Etc.

sustainable and profitable business. There are plenty of opportunities to do so because the market for their product exists. They also have the technical capabilities – being world leaders in the relevant software. However, they lack sales and marketing skills and financial capital. The Strategy Triangle provides a simple framework to summarise their situation.

While the Strategy Triangle is helpful for a high-level discussion, it has a potential weakness: it can easily allow sloppy thinking to go unchallenged. Hence it is best used as a brainstorming tool, or with a team who are truly expert, or as a way of summarising the situation after a decent amount of analysis has been conducted.

To encourage more rigorous thinking, a popular alternative is the Strategy Matrix (also known as the McKinsey or GE matrix) – as shown in the following for British Airways.

In this example, BA is competing in four segments – each shown as a circle. The average segment profitability for all competitors is shown by its positioning on the vertical axis. Segment size is indicated by the size of the circle (which can also be coloured to show the market growth of the segment). Competitive advantage is shown by the position along the horizontal axis.

The figure suggests that BA has a relatively attractive position regarding its flights to North America and other intercontinental destinations (its main focus for growth).

The strategy matrix for BA

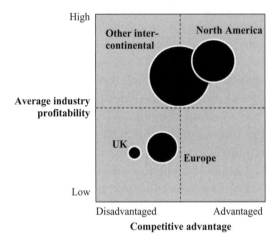

It has weaknesses in the highly competitive UK and European markets (where it has been retrenching and cutting costs). All aspects of this assessment can be supported by more detailed analysis and facts using the tools and frameworks described earlier.

This matrix is a development of the famous Boston Consulting Group matrix, which had growth rate in place of average industry profitability, and market share in place of competitive advantage. The BCG matrix was a revolutionary strategy tool in its time and is appealing because the dimensions can be quantified (although there is always an argument about the definition of the relevant market to use to come up with market share) However, one of its underlying assumptions – that market share is a guarantee of competitive advantage – is regarded as too simplistic in today's business environment.

The strategy matrix provides a high-level summary of many of the issues addressed in the external and internal assessment of the situation. Notable exceptions are the objectives of the organisation (the Strategy Triangle is better for that) and what is going on in the broader environment (although this is reflected indirectly in the assessment of segment profitability, size and growth).

A REALITY CHECK: WHAT IS ACTUAL PERFORMANCE?

One of the challenges of strategic analysis is that it often requires making judgments that cannot be proven, at least not without an unreasonable amount of data and analysis. Therefore check whether your assessment makes sense by asking whether it is consistent with actual performance. For example, if you conclude from the analysis that you are a very strong competitor in a very attractive market, you would expect to be performing well.

Note that performance, like strategy, should be analysed at the <u>segment</u> level. Overall measures of performance are better than nothing, but not by much. Also, a range of metrics should be used. The right mix will vary,

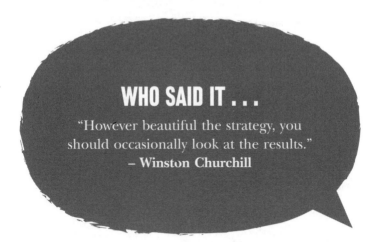

WHO SAID IT . . .

"However beautiful the strategy, you should occasionally look at the results."
– Winston Churchill

but is typically a combination of financial, strategic, and operational.

Financial metrics are the most common. The most relevant are the profitability ratios rather than liquidity or financial leverage ratios (which have more to do with financial than business strategy).

It can be useful to create a Value Tree that breaks out financial performance at progressively finer levels of detail. The exact tree will vary by industry (and the availability of data). An example, for a consumer product, is shown in the following diagram.

Ideally, the metrics should be chosen so that they can be measured and benchmarked against the competition in

Example of a Simple Value Tree

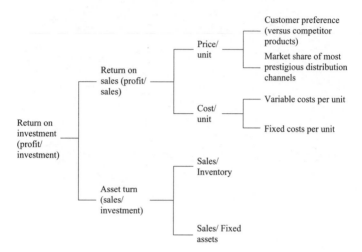

order to throw maximum light on whether or not the organisation is performing well.

Strategic metrics include:

▶ Market and segment attractiveness (market size, growth rates, average levels of profitability).

▶ Competitive success (e.g. market share and trends in market share, brand image and reputation, mystery shopper rating, relative price point, share of sales from recent products).

▶ Performance from the perspective of stakeholders other than shareholders (e.g. number of safety incidents, public opinion about the organisation, results of employee surveys).

► Forward-looking indicators (e.g. products in the pipeline, size and quality of the talent pool).

Operational metrics are typically highly customised, so the examples that follow are illustrative only:

► Capacity utilisation, strength of the wholesale network and advertising spend for the beer industry.
► Costs per sales call, customer churn rate, value per sale, and conversion rates for sales-oriented businesses.
► Operating cost per MWhour of production, availability during peak hours and efficiency of conversion of fuel to energy for a power plant.

A challenge involved in measuring performance is that sometimes the strategy delivers results which are far out in the future. For example, a nuclear power plant will take 10 years to build and bring on line, so it is necessary to be thoughtful about what metrics will provide a reasonable measure of the value generated today. Indeed power generation companies often use net present value (the value of future cash flows) to assess whether their current strategies and investments are likely to create value over their lifetime.

What happens if performance is different from what was anticipated from the strategic assessment – for example, if a business that you think has a strong competitive position is losing money? It is possible your strategic assessment is wrong. It is also possible that something is causing the organisation to perform above or below the level that its strategic position merits. For example, strongly positioned businesses may be failing to deliver good financial performance because someone other than the shareholder is getting the value (e.g. employees, unions, pensioners, customers). Alternatively, operations may be very inefficient (as with the US automotive companies in the 1980s). In such cases, the priority should be to fix the operational problems before moving on to develop a new strategy.

WHAT YOU NEED TO READ

▶ W. Chan Kim and Renée Mauborgne's *Blue Ocean Strategy*, Harvard Business School Press, 2005, is a popular strategy text which particularly emphasises the importance of creating value for customers.

▶ For a discussion of sources of competitive advantage, see various chapters in Robert Grant, *Contemporary Strategy Analysis* and *Lords of Strategy* by Walter Kiechel III, Harvard Business Press, 2010.

▶ A useful way to understand how different sources of advantage link together and deliver higher performance is to use 'systems thinking'. Books on this include *The Fifth Discipline* by Peter Senge, Random House, 1993 and *Strategic Management Dynamics*, John Wiley & Sons Ltd and *Strategy Dynamics Essentials* (eBook from *www.strategydynamics.com*) – both by Kim Warren.

▶ For more reading on mission and objectives, consult *A Sense of Mission* by Andrew Campbell and Sally Yeung, Economist Books/Hutchinson, 1990, or *Creating a Sense of Mission*, Long Range Planning, Vol 24, No 4, August 1991.

▶ For general information on financial ratios, see *Contemporary Strategy Analysis* by Grant, Chapter 2 'Putting Performance Analysis Into Practice'. Richard Koch's *Guide to Strategy* also provides some interesting examples.

IF YOU ONLY REMEMBER ONE THING

Successful strategies are founded on a rich understanding of your own situation.

CHAPTER 4
EVOLUTION

WHAT IT'S ALL ABOUT

► Why uncertainties are tricky

► Generating a list of potential uncertainties

► Modelling how uncertainties might evolve

► Prioritising uncertainties

► Summarising

Strategies have to work in the future – not the past. They have to be chosen not just on the basis of the current situation, but on how that situation might evolve, even if the future is highly uncertain and unpredictable. This poses a significant problem for strategic decision makers: they must make major choices without knowing how they will play out. This chapter explains how to think about uncertainty in a systematic way by understanding its roots and its potential effects, and then thinking through which sources of uncertainty need to be addressed when creating the strategy.

TRICKY UNCERTAINTY

An uncertainty is any aspect of the future development of the external or internal environment that cannot be reasonably predicted. *Strategic* uncertainties are those that can potentially have a big impact on the success of a strategy.

The concept of uncertainty may seem obvious but its effects are often underestimated and its upside often ignored. Frequently, the most critical uncertainties are not even considered during the design of a strategy.

Uncertainty can sometimes be relatively easy to deal with. For example, the UK supermarket chain Tesco can make a reasonable estimate of customer demand for food next year. Other forms of uncertainty such as potential price-cutting campaigns by Tesco's competitors are less easy to predict. However, these 'known unknowns' can at least be anticipated, even if the way they will unfold cannot be precisely foreseen.

But others are very difficult to anticipate. For example, few banks foresaw the extent of the global financial crisis. Not only did they underestimate the probability of such an event, but many of them felt that such a meltdown was impossible. Such seismic 'unknown unknowns' are not completely unpredictable but the smart decision-makers involved appear not to have recognised their potential significance. A normal, all-too-human response to uncertainty is to either ignore it or pretend that the future is more certain than it really is.

Uncertainty is not always a bad thing. In fact, most major opportunities for growth come from unpredicted changes seized upon by those quick enough to respond. Understanding how the situation may evolve provides plenty of upsides – not just bad news.

When designing a strategy, more time and thought need to be devoted to considering the effects of uncertainty than is commonly spent in most organisations.

WHO SAID IT . . .

"... there are also unknown unknowns – the ones we don't know we don't know."
– **Donald Rumsfeld**

OVERALL APPROACHES TO DEALING WITH UNCERTAINTY

How can the 'uncertainty paradox' – that decision-makers must make major choices without knowing how they will play out – be dealt with? One approach is to conclude that it is pointless to pretend that the future can be predicted. Instead, pick an option that provides some flexibility and be ready to adapt. Unfortunately, even this requires the strategist to think through what kind of adaptation might be required and how much to invest in being flexible.

Another approach – the one taken here – assumes that although the future is unpredictable, you can still prepare for it. You can make an educated guess about how the situation may evolve and then pick options which are likely to succeed in the most likely futures (and have a chance of surviving in the others). You cannot eliminate the effect of good or bad luck, but you can be prepared to deal with it – thereby increasing your chances of turning a potential threat into an opportunity.

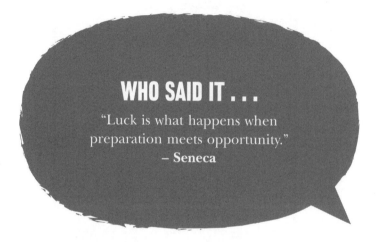

WHO SAID IT . . .

"Luck is what happens when preparation meets opportunity."
– **Seneca**

The simplest way is to use your intuition: think of alternative futures, how the key uncertainties might play out and what you can do about it. If you need a little help, a more systematic approach is shown in the following chart. You don't have to work through all the steps in detail. Fortunately, you can 'pick and mix' different elements, doing some steps intuitively and some analytically.

Start on the left by describing the current situation using the tools and frameworks detailed in the previous two

Projecting how the situation may evolve

Describe current situation (previous chapters)

Generate list of potential uncertainties

Optional: Analyse broader trends or select relevant analogies to suggest how uncertainties may evolve

Model how uncertainties might evolve

Iterate for most important uncertainties

Prioritise the uncertainties based on their impact

Summarise how the future might evolve and major uncertainties

Design and select options in the light of potential uncertainties (next chapter)

chapters. Then turn to the steps in the middle box, which are the ones covered in this chapter.

First, generate a long list of potential uncertainties – for example, the growth rate of customer demand. Then model how these uncertainties might evolve. For example, you could model the number of customers and the demand per customer, concluding that demand might grow 5% to 10% per annum.

Now prioritise the uncertainties by evaluating their potential impact. For example, demand levels could significantly affect profitability because the organisation has very high fixed costs – in which case, changes in demand would rank high on the list. Finally, synthesise your analysis into a view of how the future might evolve and the main uncertainties to plan for.

In the rest of this chapter we describe tools and approaches that can be used to support each of these steps in analysing uncertainty.

GENERATING A LIST OF POTENTIAL UNCERTAINTIES

To generate a list of uncertainties that might affect the outcome of the strategy, you can simply ask yourself: How might the situation evolve, and what are the uncertainties? If there is a risk that you will not think broadly

WHO YOU NEED TO KNOW
Nassim Taleb

Nassim Taleb (born 1960) grew up in the Lebanon, receiving, in that unlucky country, an education in unpredictability. A former senior Wall Street trader, risk expert, and university professor in risk engineering, he is most famous for his best-selling book, *The Black Swan*, in which he posits that the most significant changes that affect organisations and lives are the unknown unknowns. For example, he describes discussions with the management of the MGM Mirage casino in Las Vegas, which 'spent hundreds of millions of dollars on gambling theory and high-tech surveillance, while the bulk of the risks came from outside their models,' – such as the white tiger that mauled magician Roy Horn in October 2003, costing the casino $100 million.

Perfectly timed, *The Black Swan* was published as the global financial crisis broke.

Like Henry Mintzberg, Taleb provides an antidote to the over-confidence shown by some sections of the strategy industry, which put too much faith in plans and the predictions of experts. In his own words, 'My major hobby is teasing people who take themselves and the quality of their knowledge too seriously, and those who don't have the courage to sometimes say: I don't know . . .'

enough, stimulate your thinking by considering *different categories of uncertainty.*

One way of categorising uncertainty is according to time-frames. Consider the example of a strategic decision to invest in a coal-fired power plant. Think about the uncertainties that might prevail in a one, one-year and a 15-year timeframe. A short-term uncertainty is whether you can obtain a permit for the plant and whether the grid company will agree to connect you to the power grid. A medium-term uncertainty is the price of the power you sell into the power market. Long-term uncertainties include whether government regulations will ultimately close coal-fired plants due to their high carbon dioxide emissions. In this way you will generate a more comprehensive list of uncertainties than if you just use intuition (which may tend to focus on just the short, or the long-term – depending on your mindset).

Note that the definitions of short-term vs. long-term will depend on the nature of the strategy and the sector. For an energy company, the long-term might be 15 to 30 years out, but if you're developing a plan for a line of fashion clothing, long-term might be 12 months.

Another way to categorise uncertainties is to think about strategic uncertainties associated with the concepts introduced in earlier chapters about the external environment and internal situation – such as uncertainties about attractiveness and competitive advantage. The following are illustrated with examples related to an investment in a coal-fired power plant:

▶ Uncertainties about *segmentation*. What industries and segments might emerge, grow, combine, decline and die? For example, in the long run petrol retailing and power distribution may combine if electric vehicles win significant market share.
▶ Uncertainties about *segment attractiveness* (size, growth and profitability). Size and growth of power markets are relatively predictable but

there is considerable uncertainty about future prices and thus profits, because these are affected by hard-to-predict factors such as the degree of over- or under-capacity in the power market.

► Uncertainties about *what customers and other stakeholders value*. For example, how will the local community react to the installation of the plant? Will they welcome the boost to the local economy or have concerns about potential pollution or safety incidents?

► Uncertainties about *competitive advantage*. The future competitiveness of the plant is uncertain because the price of coal and the level of taxes on carbon emissions are hard to predict.

A third way to categorise uncertainty is by degrees of unpredictability, for example, 'relatively predictable', 'known unknowns' and 'unknown unknowns'. In the case of the power plant, demand for power is 'relatively predictable'. Uncertainties such as the power price, the community's feelings about the plant, and the response of competitors are 'known unknowns' – you know these are uncertainties but cannot accurately predict how they will evolve with any degree of accuracy.

Unknown unknowns are things that you have not even thought of. By definition, they are difficult to grasp – but it is possible. Brainstorm for uncertainties that have not yet been considered in your strategic assessment, such as the development of a new power technology that could undermine the competitiveness of existing technologies, or a step change in geo-politics that could affect the security of certain fuel supplies, with knock-on effects for the power industry. By doing so, you will have turned an 'unknown unknown' into a 'known unknown'.

SCENARIOS

An alternative to this rather reductionist approach to uncertainty is to generate different scenarios of how the future might evolve.

A scenario represents a logically consistent and holistic view of a potential future state. It helps identify the most important uncertainties and how they might evolve. Furthermore, it often provides a broader view of how the future may evolve than thinking about specific uncertainties. For example, in discussing the power plant investment, you may come up with three scenarios:

1. 'Business as normal' – in which coal plants are competitive on costs, and in which the opportunity to expand the plant is granted.
2. 'Frustration' – in which the plant does not incur higher costs but cannot expand due to resistance from other stakeholders such as the local community or the grid company.
3. 'Green world' in which all coal plants suffer penal carbon taxes and have to be shut down.

From these scenarios you can see that there are two big uncertainties. The first is a mix of environmental and technological pressures which might raise the cost of coal plants, forcing them to close or operate with lower margins. The second is whether you will get permission to expand the initial power plant investment due to resistance from the local community or the grid company.

This illustrates a number of points to remember about scenarios. The first is that they should capture the most important uncertainties. The second is that it is best to have relatively few scenarios – otherwise the whole process becomes very complex. Finally, the point is not to try and predict which of these scenarios is the most likely, because any of them might credibly occur. The final strategy, therefore, should ideally work in all three.

WHO SAID IT . . .

"You know nothing for sure . . . except the fact that you know nothing for sure."
– **President John F. Kennedy**

Scenarios are a powerful way to identify important uncertainties. They can be particularly helpful if you are developing strategy in a group, or need to communicate the strategy to a large number of people. They serve to open up people's minds if they are finding it difficult to imagine why the current strategy needs to be changed. A scenario is not just an analytical tool but a way of challenging existing thought and provoking debate.

MODELLING EVOLUTION

By this stage you have generated an overly long list of uncertainties. The next stage is to prioritise. You may be able to do this intuitively or the answer may be instantly obvious. If not, you should first model how the uncertainties might evolve, then prioritise the uncertainties on the basis of their potential impact on the outcome of the strategy.

There are a number of different ways of modelling uncertainty. Sometimes, quantitative modelling is possible. For example, to model uncertainty about the demand for power you might simply look at predictions about population levels (which tend to be reasonably reliable) and multiply these by estimated usage of energy per capita (also reasonably reliable).

Quantitative modelling can be more sophisticated than simply multiplying two numbers together. For example, computer models can predict power prices on the basis of changes in demand, future fuel prices, the amount and type of power plant capacity available, and the operating characteristics of all the individual power plants in the region. They use inputs such as the price of fuel to provide a probability distribution of expected power prices.

Such modelling requires that you have all the data you need to make a projection. But what if you don't? For example, to run a computer programme that predicts power prices will require estimates of future fuel prices which may not be available. One alternative is to use a qualitative approach, looking at broader trends or analogies, and using them to derive qualitative projections of how fuel prices might evolve.

For example, projections of global energy demand growth and of the availability of energy supplies reveal that there is lots of coal in the world but a finite amount of oil – and that much of the oil is controlled by OPEC. Also, demand for oil is rising faster than the growth in oil reserves (oil that is still in the ground). So you may hypothesise that long-term coal prices will rise at close to the level of inflation but oil prices will rise faster. Armed with these general predictions you can turn to making predictions about changes in power prices using the computer programme.

However, at other times a quantitative model is not available or possible to create. In these cases there are techniques that help you model how the uncertainties may evolve – some of the more popular ones are discussed over the next few sections.

BROADER TRENDS

PESTLE analysis, described in Chapter 2, can be a useful way to think about uncertainties related to broader trends in the macro environment – by thinking about how Political, Economic, Social, Technological, Legal and Environmental trends might evolve. Data on these trends are usually available and can be applied to consider how a more specific uncertainty might evolve.

For example, consider the uncertainty about whether coal-fired power stations will be allowed to operate in the future. Environmental trends could lead to pressure for the closure of coal-powered stations. Legal and regulatory history suggests that existing coal-fired stations will not be forced to close by fiat, but that extra charges may be imposed on them that could lead to a similar outcome. On the other hand, Technological trends suggest that there may be ways to store the carbon dioxide that coal stations produce, and that alternative power sources such as wind and solar will not fully meet the needs of customers due to the intermittent nature of their output. Economic trends also suggest that the relatively low cost of coal-fired plants offers some advantage over wind and solar. By thinking about how these PESTLE trends may evolve it is possible to see how the specific uncertainties around the survival of coal plants might develop.

Country risk analysis – a version of PESTLE analysis – can be used in a similar fashion to structure an exploration of what the future may hold in a particular country if, for example, you were planning to build a coal plant in Indonesia.

Analysing broader trends like this may require some highly customised work. For example, imagine that the development of wind power is one of your key uncertainties. You will need information about current technology, suppliers, production and operating costs, regulation and subsidy regimes and how all of these might develop over time. Such an exercise will require significant resources, careful planning and thorough data collection and analysis.

INDUSTRY ANALOGIES

Analysing broader trends to project how uncertainties may evolve can be a major undertaking. A more focused approach is to think of a relevant analogy to the situation. The idea is to think 'How might uncertainties unfold if my situation developed in the same way as in this analogy'. For example, returning to the coal-fired power station example, if the uncertainty you are concerned about is the development of the wind turbine business, and you used the analogy of the development of the motor car and the emergence of Ford as the market leader, you might think of how the many different manufacturers of wind turbines today might consolidate down to one or two producers using mass production techniques to produce standardised turbines at ever lower costs – increasing their competitiveness.

The trick here is to identify an analogy that matches the particular situation you are trying to analyse. There are many analogies available – some of the most commonly used are briefly described here; more about each can be discovered using the references at the end of the chapter.

Substitution curves. When a new technology or product begins to substitute for an existing technology or product it often follows a predictable relationship, known as a 'substitution curve' (the exact relationship is shown as a footnote in the following figure). Plotting the historic substitution curve allows you to see if the effect is occurring in your industry. If so, it can be used to make a projection of future substitution – assuming that the trend continues on the same line.

There is one important caveat: the trend may not continue for ever – at some point the substitution effect may stop. The example in the following chart illustrates this point. The curve shows that synthetic fibres (the 'new' product) substituted for natural fibres (the 'old' product) but when the ratio of new to old exceeded 50% the trend stopped (it actually reversed for a while before continuing again).

Substitution curve for fibres

The ratio in usage of <u>Synthetic fibres</u>
<u>Natural fibres</u>

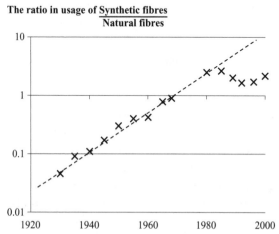

Note: The graph plots log(f/1-f) over time, where f is the fraction of total demand achieved by the new technology or product.

From: *Predictions 10 years later*, Theodore Modis, Used with the pemission of the author.

In the power industry, substitution curves might be used to evaluate the rate of adoption of new technologies, such as wind power and energy-saving light bulbs. Just make sure that you consider whether the substitution effect might stop at some point. For example, wind power is unlikely to meet 100% of power needs because it only operates when the wind blows and so requires more reliable sources of power to complement it.

Product and industry life cycles. Products and industries tend to go through predictable trends or stages. A typical cycle would be introduction, growth, maturity and decline. For example, coal-fired power stations are mature products (although some revolutionary new designs are being tested), while wind power is in a growth phase, and solar power in the introductory phase. Use of the life cycle analogy suggests that coal may at some point go into decline, wind will mature and solar may take off into a higher growth phase at some point.

Disruptive technologies. Clayton Christensen, a Harvard Business School professor, created this term to describe 'a process by which a product or service takes root initially in simple applications at the bottom of a market and then relentlessly moves 'up market', eventually displacing established competitors'. One example would be the Japanese motorcycle companies (Honda and Yamaha) who started by gaining a foothold at the bottom of the market with cheaper bikes, and then worked their way upwards, disrupting and eventually displacing UK competitors who had higher costs.

According to Christensen, this is a common feature of many industries. It explains how established incumbents with strong competitive positions can be unseated. Organisations should consider whether such a trend might affect their own industry, providing an opportunity to displace a strong competitor or bringing the threat of an unexpected new entrant. Use of this analogy might suggest that solar could become a disruptive technology if, for example, the Sahara could provide enough power to serve a huge portion of Europe's demand.

Deconstruction. Another analogy, highly relevant in the internet age, is that of industry deconstruction, whereby previously vertically-integrated industries break up. An example is personal computers, where the previous vertical integration typified by Apple and IBM in the 1970s and 80s gave way to a highly deconstructed industry where chips are now provided by specialists such as Intel, operating systems by Microsoft, software packages by a range of providers, and PC assembly by low-cost operators such as Dell or Lenovo. Telecommunications and many previously regulated industries have also deconstructed in response to a mix of global, economic and regulatory changes.

Some industries may re-construct – for example, in the UK, the vertically integrated national electric utility was broken up into separate generators and distribution companies which have largely re-integrated over time into a set of vertically-integrated companies.

DIY analogies. In some situations it can be helpful to develop your own analogies. For example, for a company facing a new competitor from China, or the challenge of going international, or deregulation of their industry, it may be informative to look at how other companies and industries in similar circumstances have developed. Get creative!

BEHAVIOUR

A form of uncertainty that is difficult to model is a change in the behaviour of actors such as customers, stakeholders or competitors. An analysis of a variety of broad trends can be combined to indirectly model how *customer behaviour* might change over time, e.g.:

- ▶ demographic changes (age, country of birth, marital status, social class);
- ▶ social and economic changes (e.g. disposable income, health);
- ▶ lifestyle trends (e.g. availability and use of leisure time, aspirations);
- ▶ typical hopes and fears (e.g. feelings about crime, protection of children, unemployment).

For example, consider the uncertainties surrounding how customers in a developing country chose between different brands of detergent. Broad *economic* trends suggest that consumers are getting richer. *Social* trends suggest that they are also getting busier and value their free time more highly. Together these trends suggest that consumers might pay a premium for a detergent that saves them time – for example because it does not require a pre-wash.

Investigating broader trends enables you to indirectly model specific uncertainties. But such analyses must typically be highly customised. If you want to understand how purchasers of machine tools will change their buying behaviour you will need a very different analysis from that for consumers of detergents.

Understanding *competitive behaviour* can also be very important, particularly in concentrated industries where competitors' actions can have a significant impact on the outcome of a strategy. Often this is done intuitively, but there are techniques that can be used to model how competitors may behave.

A common approach is *role-play*, which could be as simple as putting yourself in the shoes of your competitor and imagining what you would do. It can be done as a thought exercise with parallel studying of published data, or as a more elaborate group exercise.

More developed forms of role-play are often described as 'war games', due to their use by the armed forces. In a classic military example, the 'blue team' plays the role of their own side, and the 'red team' plays the role of the enemy. The teams come up with a plan of what to do, with the red team trying to be as aggressive and radical as possible. Rules, computer programmes and referees are used in various combinations to determine the potential outcomes of different strategies.

Returning to our power industry example, if the power plant were reliant on getting access to the power grid,

Examples of uncertainties and modelled effect

Uncertainty	Techniques used to model effect	Implications of modelling
Whether permit will be granted	• Role play of community and power plant	• Could potentially block future expansion of plant but highly uncertain how this will play out
Effect of resistance by grid company to power plant	• Wargame involving grid company, power plant and regulator	• Likely to delay operation of the plant
Demand for power	• Projected growth in population • Historical development of power usage per capita	• Increasing with some cyclicality
Fuel prices	• Broad trends in energy industry	• Coal prices rise with inflation • Oil price rises at a higher rate
Development of wind power	• Analogy to history of the automotive industry and specifically the emergence of Ford	• Likely consolidation of suppliers and reduction in costs and prices
Development of solar power	• Disruptive technology analogy	• Solar could be a major player but future is highly uncertain
Power prices	• Computer modelling using scenarios for fuel prices, projected supply/demand balance and projected development of wind and solar as inputs	• Attractive prices under most scenarios
Forced closure of all CO_2 emitting power plants	• PESTLE analysis	• Conflicting trends lead to a high level of uncertainty

and the grid operator were itself a competitor in power generation, you could run a role-play or wargame in which three teams played the power plant, the grid company and the regulator, respectively. Those representing the power plant and the grid company might come up with arguments to put to the regulator, and propose actions (that serve their own interests). The team playing the regulator would then make a judgement. Role-play can be done quickly in a small group or played out over several weeks. It can involve a couple of close colleagues or extend to include outsiders such as people who previously worked for the regulator or for competitors.

PRIORITISING UNCERTAINTIES

You now have a long list of uncertainties whose potential evolution you have modelled in various ways (see the table opposite for the power plant example). You need to prioritise those which are the most important for your strategy to deal with.

A typical tool to structure your thinking is the matrix overleaf (for simplicity, only four uncertainties from the power plant example have been shown). A useful idea to introduce here is that of the 'base case' – a credible way in which the environment and thus strategy might evolve. The uncertainties can be thought of in terms of the *probability* that they deviate from the base case, and the potential *impact* of them doing so. In the case of an uncertainty such as, 'whether there would be a forced closure of all CO_2 emitting power plants', the base case is 'No'. The probability of a deviation from the base case ('Yes') is low, but the impact of any deviation would be very high.

If uncertainties in the bottom right have a negative impact, such as this one, then it would be ideal to insure against them or hedge them – for example by investing in renewables. If they have a large upside (such as 'the site can be used for commercial development after the life time of the plant'), the option to exploit those uncertainties (for example, by being able to redevelop the site) should be retained where feasible.

Uncertainties in the top right are the most important to manage, mitigating the downside whilst trying to retain the option of capturing any upside. It may be necessary to build the strategy around such uncertainties. For example, if the grid company could block the power plant then it might be worth selling a share of the business to that company.

The effect of uncertainties in the top left must be understood but can generally be tolerated. However, it is important to have the operational ability to adapt the strategy in real time as things change. Uncertainties in the bottom left can typically be ignored.

Prioritisation of uncertainties

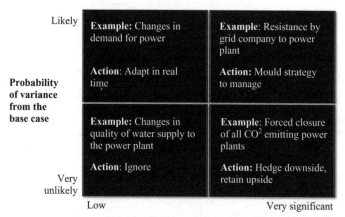

Potential Impact of variance from the base case

A classic approach is to start by using your intuition to position the different uncertainties, refining your thinking as you do more analysis. This enables you to focus on what appear to be the most important uncertainties. As the analysis progresses, the prioritisation is revised and the work re-focused accordingly.

You now know what the main uncertainties are, the probability of them varying from the base case, and the impact that such variance might have. You are thus in a position to think through how the organisation might perform in a range of possible futures. Designing and choosing the right strategy option is the next step.

WHO YOU NEED TO KNOW
Don Sull

Don Sull is a Professor at the London Business School, who previously worked as a consultant at McKinsey & Company, and at private equity investment firm Clayton, Dubilier & Rice. He is also an active investor in several technology start-ups.

Sull's early research described the self-imposed difficulties companies face in dealing with change. It highlighted the self-imposed 'blinders' that conceal what is going on in the external environment, and the routinised processes, webs of relationships and dogmas that prevent companies changing.

His more recent research assumes change and uncertainty as a given and focuses on what to do about it. Noting the obstacles that stop large organisations evolving effectively

– some thrive on change while others fail to adapt – he attributes survival to a combination of agility (the ability to adapt to change) and absorption (the ability to survive tough times).

Sull is one of the few with something to say about the tricky area of whether and how organisations built up to be successful in one world, can succeed in another.

WHAT YOU NEED TO READ

▶ *Strategy Under Uncertainty* by Hugh Courtney, Jane Kirkland, and Patrick Viguerie in the McKinsey Quarterly, June 2000, provides an overview of types of uncertainty and how to deal with them.

▶ Don Sull's series of articles in the *Harvard Business Review* include 'Why good companies go bad' (July/August 1999), 'Strategy as Active Waiting' (September 2005) and 'How to Thrive in Turbulent Markets' (February 2009).

▶ There is a wealth of information on scenario planning on the web, for example, via the Shell website (*www.shell.com/home/content/aboutshell/our_strategy*) and at www.mindofafox.com.

▶ Country risk analysis, technology forecasting and war games are covered in chapters in *Business and Competitive Analysis* by C. Fleisher and B. Bensoussan, FT Press, 2007.

▶ Information on product and industry life cycles can be found in *Contemporary Strategy Analysis* by Robert Grant, Anita McGahan's

'Explanation of the Four Trajectories of Industry Change' which can be reviewed at www.12manage.com, and *Dealing with Darwin* by Geoffrey Moore (of 'Moore's Law' fame).

▶ Disruptive technologies are discussed at *www.claytonchristensen.com/disruptive_innovation.html*.

▶ Benefiting from the upsides of uncertainty is discussed in *Strategy as Options on the Future* by Peter J. Williamson, Sloan Management Review, Vol 40, No 3, Spring 1999, pp. 117–126.

IF YOU ONLY REMEMBER ONE THING

Make sure your strategy will succeed in an uncertain future.

CHAPTER 5

ISSUES AND OPTIONS

WHAT IT'S ALL ABOUT

- ► The power of framing
- ► Generating new frames
- ► Narrowing the frame
- ► Generating new options
- ► Evaluating options
- ► Iterating the framing–options cycle

You have done much of the heavy lifting. You have ana-lysed the situation and how it might evolve. The next step is to identify the most attractive options and choose between them.

Occasionally this is an easy task. The issues are self-evident and there is an obvious and practical option for the organisation to achieve its objectives. More com-monly, things are not so clear. It may be that there are too many options, or widely varying views on what the best options are. These can be overwhelming for a team to analyse, and lead to arguments and friction.

In other cases it can appear that there are too few options. Perhaps none of the options are very attractive, or none really address the underlying threats and prob-lems. Or else the team seems to be thinking too narrowly about what is possible. There may be attractive short-term options but no clarity about where to go over the long-term, or plenty of ideas about where to go in the long-term with no suitable pathways available in the short-term.

In short, you sometimes need to generate more options and sometimes to constrain them to a more manageable and focused number.

To *generate more options*, the most direct approach is to conduct a brainstorming session. For example, if your organisation is suffering from flat sales and profits, you could simply ask everyone to come up with at least three ideas for growing the business. Another approach – less direct but often more potent – is to redefine or reframe the situation in such a way that opens up new options.

'Framing' involves defining an issue in a way that defines a boundary for the options to be considered. For example, instead of framing the issue as 'What are the opportunities to grow?' you could frame the situation as 'How do we double the value of the company?' This alternative widens the boundaries on the options that can be considered, generating a broader range of ideas than the initial frame – for example, ways to increase profitability by cutting costs as well as ways of growing sales.

To *focus the generation of options* you could specify options of a particular type – for example, 'Ways to redesign core products', or frame the situation more narrowly, such as asking 'How do we increase sales of our core product lines by 20% within a year?' or 'Which new countries could we expand into?'

Developing a strategy often requires you to do a bit of broadening and a bit of narrowing – generating more ways to frame the situation and more options at some stages, and narrowing down at others. How to do so is the main topic of this chapter. The emphasis will be on how to generate more frames and options, because this is typically more difficult than narrowing down.

It is important to emphasise that the process of framing the issue, generating options, evaluating them and then picking one should not be practiced as a sequence of discrete activities. Instead it should be an *iterative cycle* of framing, generating and evaluating options and re-framing to generate new and improved options – a topic that we will return to at the end of the chapter.

THE POWER OF FRAMING

Framing is often the crux of a strategic decision, but its importance is frequently overlooked. It will determine the options that you consider and the criteria that you use to select between options. Conversely, inappropriate framing is likely to lead to the wrong option. But framing is often done without enough thought and debate. Indeed, it often occurs at an unconscious level – people do not even realise that they have automatically framed the situation in a particular way. Therefore it can be helpful to have some tools to help you generate and evaluate alternative frames.

To illustrate the importance of framing, imagine that you were the head of the NATO military mission in Afghanistan in 2010. The issue facing you could be framed in various ways, e.g.:

1. How to defeat the Taliban and al-Qaeda.
2. How to create a stable Afghanistan.
3. How to make a graceful exit within two years.

A team of military officers might naturally focus on options for securing a military victory, because they will intuitively frame the issue as 'How to defeat the Taliban and al-Qaeda'. Only if they re-frame the issue as 'How to create a stable Afghanistan' might they begin to think about options that do not rely purely on a military victory. Switching frames (or, to use another related metaphor, thinking outside the box) is notoriously difficult but also very powerful.

For a business example of the power of framing and re-framing, consider a story told by Jack Welch, former CEO of General Electric, a major US company. He had insisted that the heads of all the business units within GE make their businesses number 1 or 2 in their industry. Unfortunately, a side effect was that the business heads framed the boundaries of their industry narrowly to max-imise their market share, allowing their businesses to be defined as the industry leader. This led them to be overly conservative and ignore options that required them to grow in new markets where they could not immediately be a market leader.

Welch then asked all the business heads to re-draw the boundaries of their businesses in such a way that they had less than 10% market share. By doing so, he made them re-frame the boundaries of their industry and the growth options available. The business heads had origi-nally framed their objective as 'Become number 1 or 2 within a narrowly defined industry.' Welch encouraged them to re-frame the goal as 'Grow my business to become number 1 or 2 in a much larger industry.' As a result, '. . . over the next five years, we doubled our top-line growth rate at GE with the same yet newly energized portfolio of businesses.'

GENERATING NEW FRAMES

As already discussed, it is natural for the brain to select a particular frame and thus a narrow set of options. One way to broaden the set of options considered is to generate a range of alternative frames – each of which triggers its own set of options. How do you do this?

Most frames consist of a suggested strategic objective, such as 'Defeat the Taliban', and sometimes a constraint such as 'Within two years'. So, one way to generate alternative frames is to list alternative objectives and constraints, and then create different strategic questions by combining the two lists – for example, 'Defeat the Taliban within two years' could become 'Create a stable Afghanistan within two years' or 'Defeat the Taliban within 10 years' or 'Create a stable Afghanistan within 10 years' – each of which has a different set of associated options.

Another way of coming up with alternative framings is to think of ways of making the current framing of the issue broader or narrower. So, for example, consider the framing 'How to defeat the Taliban, with acceptable losses.' This could be made *broader* by stating the objective as 'How to maintain peace in the Near East while maintaining popular support back home', or *narrower* by asking 'How to get control of Helmand province without losing more than 200 troops.' Surprisingly, narrow frames can actually generate new options because the narrow frame can require more creative options. For example, the narrower framing above, requiring the loss of no more than 200 troops could lead to new ideas about how to limit the need for armed confrontation by negotiating with the Taliban.

New frames can also emerge by probing whether you have got to the real issue, using the '5 Whys' technique. Switching to a business example, suppose you have a problem employee who is failing to perform. You might ask 'Why are they failing to perform?' and come back with the answer 'Because they have too much to do.' Why do they have too much to do?': 'Because you have allowed the business to grow without adding enough staff.' Now the strategic issue becomes 'How to add staff' – rather than 'How to fire the problem employee.' To delve into the root cause of a problem you need to ask 'Why' five times – at which point you will either have got to the true issue or have exhausted everyone's patience.

Another way to generate more frames is a scenario-planning exercise, creating several alternative future environments. Each will yield different issues for the organisation and varying frames – for example, 'being ready to take advantage of a growing market' or 'fighting off new competitors'.

NARROWING THE FRAME

It might seem that generating new frames and options is always desirable. In reality, it is hard for any one individual or group to handle too many ideas. Narrowing down can focus the strategy process. This can be useful early on in a project if you are in danger of 'boiling the ocean' with excessive analysis, or later, when you are running out of time and need to focus in on a shortlist of options.

The challenge is how to narrow the frame without blinding yourself to potentially attractive options.

WHO SAID IT . . .

"Each man should frame life so that at some future hour fact and his dreaming meet."
– Victor Hugo

As the quotation suggests, a valuable frame typically has two characteristics. It is grounded in the facts, while also reflecting the overall mission or – as Victor Hugo so eloquently put it – the 'dream'. This suggests that a sensible way to narrow down the range of frames is to select ones that reflect both the mission/objective of the organisation and the realities of the pathways available (what Hugo meant by 'fact').

For example, the mission of NATO is to maintain the security of Europe and North America. The framings 'How to defeat the Taliban' or 'How to create a stable Afghanistan' are both consistent with this. In contrast, 'How to get out within two years' appears not to be consistent because it will lead to potential insecurity in the future.

Having narrowed the frames down to a choice of two, now consider which best reflect the pathways available. Unfortunately, neither looks very achievable. Defeating the Taliban requires flushing out an enemy from notoriously rugged terrain; creating a stable Afghanistan appears no easier. Perhaps they could be combined to frame the issue as 'How to contain the Taliban, allowing Afghanistan to enjoy some economic development and the rule of law' – a formulation that is aligned with the mission and potentially achievable. In summary, you have now narrowed down the frame to one that will encourage a focused search for interesting options.

GENERATING OPTIONS

It is one of the paradoxes of strategy that it requires both the critical faculties to analyse the situation and weigh alternative strategies *and* the creative flair to generate insights and options. This does not mean that analysis is dispensable to the process, it's just that coming up with the insightful option that solves the strategic issue also requires some magic dust. A good option will almost always need to come partly from a creative insight.

With that proviso, the next sections of this chapter present some ways to stimulate your creativity. You will certainly not want to use them all – so there is also some guidance as to when they are most useful. They should be viewed as complementary rather than alternatives.

GENERATING OPTIONS FROM THE BOTTOM UP

As discussed earlier, a strategy consists of an objective or goal, and the pathway to achieve that objective – with the pathway defined by a combination of a commitment of resources, a general sense of the opportunities to be targeted along with any constraints on how resources can be deployed.

You can build a strategy option from the bottom up by simply combining alternative objectives and pathways using the analysis you have done to date and the various framings you have generated. But which should you focus on first? Should you start with a list of alternative objectives and then work out pathways to those objectives, or look at the pathways available and select objectives based on which are feasible? The answer is to use both in an iterative process so that the resulting options include the best combinations of desirable goals and feasible pathways.

One approach is to start with an objective and then think through what pathways might be available to achieve that objective – sometimes described as 'ambition driven' options. Alternative objectives can be drawn from the alternative framings you have generated; then, define alternative pathways. For example, suppose you have framed the objective in Afghanistan as 'To defeat the Taliban.' Start creating alternative pathways such as 'Use 150,000 NATO troops and cooperation with the Pakistan army (resources) to cut off the supply lines for the Taliban while systematically sweeping the Taliban out area by area (the general direction of the pathway) and minimising civilian casualties (a constraint).'

In the early stages of generating options you will want to keep the description of the pathway at a fairly high level. However, as you narrow down the range of potential strategies, there is a benefit to planning things in depth to really test out how realistic your option is (remember Seneca's advice that 'luck is what happens when preparation meets opportunity').

However much detail you decide to plan to, those responsible for implementation should be heavily involved, as they have the insight and motivation to ensure that the pathway is realistic.

Instead of starting with an objective, you could start with a feasible pathway in what is sometimes called a 'condition driven' approach – because it starts from a consideration of the current situation or condition. This can be a more pragmatic approach but tends to lead to incremental options. For example, observing the situation in Afghanistan you might consider a pathway such as 'Use the existing 100,000 US troops to gain control of some of the major Taliban controlled areas – forcing them into the mountains.' You would then need to consider the strategic objectives that would serve – such as 'Encouraging the Taliban to come to the negotiating table', and decide whether that was consistent with the overall mission.

The ambition and condition driven approaches are useful complements to each other and will typically deliver quite different sets of options.

GENERATING OPTIONS USING STRATEGY TOOLS AND FRAMEWORKS

The most viable strategy options are often incremental expansions from the existing position, as demonstrated by Chris Zook's studies of successful growth strategies.

WHO YOU NEED TO KNOW
Chris Zook

Zook holds degrees from Williams College, Harvard, and Oxford University and leads the Global Strategy Practice at Bain & Company, managing a project on growth that started in 1990. *The first book from this project, Profit from the Core,* found that nine out of ten companies that had sustained profitable growth for a decade had focused on their core businesses rather than diversification. Subsequent books looked at how to grow beyond the core, but Zook's main message is clear: In most situations, it is safest to look at options that build on the core business and sources of advantage (something he claims companies do not do rigorously enough).

In later work, Zook considered how to redefine the core and go beyond it by expanding what he describes as 'undervalued business platforms, untapped customer insights and

157

underexploited capabilities', using a process similar to the one in this book.

Zook's research has the advantage of being based on the many case studies that are available to a large management consulting firm. It offers practical wisdom based on real examples rather than theory – albeit from a consultant who makes his living selling large projects to large companies.

The strategy concepts and tools described in earlier chapters, which describe the *current* situation, can be useful as a starting point for thinking about potential *incremental* options. This is particularly helpful when you want to narrow the focus down to pragmatic options. The following are brief descriptions of how the tools described earlier might be used:

▶ *Creating new value propositions for customers.* For this you could use customer segmentation to think of new combinations of customer needs you might target. You might, for example, segment coffee shop customers to come up with a design that served the needs of a particular group such as parents with toddlers who want a break while shopping, or people who want to grab a coffee and go as soon as possible, Or you could use the value curve tool – starting with today's value curve for a coffee shop and trying to innovate new value curves to provide superior products or serve new customer segments.

▶ *Building on existing sources of advantage.* You might use the attractiveness/advantage matrix, the value chain, or the idea of building on existing capabilities and positions. You can then think about ways to use today's capabilities and sources of advantage to target new opportunities. This is useful when you have a strong advantage which could be stretched into new areas – for example, if you are Tesco or Starbucks, looking at expanding into new formats, products or countries.

▶ *Improving the attractiveness of your current markets* – using the five forces framework to think through ways you might weaken forces such as rivalry and buyer power, which reduce profitability. For example, you could use this as Starbucks to think of ways of making customers more loyal and thus less susceptible to competitors – perhaps with a loyalty card, or giving regular customers the chance to choose the music played while they are in the store.

Other frameworks that can be helpful for stimulating new options are briefly discussed here:

▶ *Multiple horizons* – a simple but powerful way to stretch your thinking. By generating options that would be appropriate for different time horizons you will be forced to arrive at quite different ideas. For example, a 12-month horizon might stimulate thinking about options to reduce manufacturing costs, a three-year horizon about building market share to become a leader in your local market, and a longer term horizon to consider whether an international or global position might eventually be required.

▶ The *Ansoff matrix* consists of a simple two-by-two matrix, with one axis for 'existing products' and 'new products', and the other for 'existing markets' and 'new markets' (customers can be substituted for markets). The idea is a simple one: each box represents a different way to grow. The matrix does not evaluate the merits of any of these options; it simply stimulates thinking about alternatives. A web search can yield further information, as will many strategy textbooks.

▶ *Who, What, How analysis* – First define your current position by defining who the customer is, what product they are being offered, and how it is produced. The next step is to think about changes to either the who, the what or the how. For example, Hertz's primary business model is to sell convenient access at airports to cars (What), to business and leisure travellers (Who), using a network of rental offices and depots (How). You might create a new option selling access to cars located near your house (What), to people who do not own cars (Who), by allowing customers to book online and use swipe cards to access cars located in parking bays on city streets (How). Indeed, Zipcar has already done this!

Further information can be found via the references at the end of the chapter.

GENERATING OPTIONS USING GENERIC STRATEGIES

Another way to increase the range of options is to consider whether any typical or 'generic' strategies might be customised to fit your particular situation. Such strategies include:

▶ *Low cost leadership* through market share, relentless improvements in operating efficiency, pressure on purchasing costs, supply chain design or product simplification and design. Examples would include Toyota in small cars, or discount supermarkets such as Aldi.

▶ *Differentiation* from providing high-value products to customers for whom product characteristics are more important than price. Approaches include creating a strong brand or reputation, attracting the best employees, being at the leading edge of technology, or controlling critical distribution channels. Examples include branded goods such as speciality vodkas, cosmetics, or services such as management consultancy.

▶ *Focus.* By targeting a particular customer or product niche, dominate it. For example, did you know that a German company Agathon is the leading producer of chocolate moulds for large-scale industrial production?

▶ *Shifting the allocation of investment to more attractive industries and segments.* If you are in many businesses it is worth seeing where the investment of money and time is going and how well it matches the positioning of the businesses on the matrix. You should be investing in businesses where you have a chance of being a strong player. Many organisations fall into the trap of investing in struggling businesses in a vain attempt to turn them around, or under-investing where they are strongest.

▶ *Capturing the value of a network.* eBay and Facebook achieved success by creating a network based on a virtual circle of winning more customers – creating a more valuable service – attracting even more customers, and so on.

▶ *Controlling an industry* (especially an unattractive one) by consolidation and vertical integration.

This strategy can pay off if it also provides concrete benefits for customers. An example is Apple in its combination of the iPod and iTunes.

▶ *Creating a collaborative network* whereby the strategy emphasises building strong links with suppliers, customers and potential customers. An example is ARM, whose computer chip technology is used in 95% of all mobile phones. It has a network or 'ecosystem' of 400 other companies and tens of thousands of developers which has enabled it to be successful in competing with Intel – a company over 40 times its size.

The generic strategies described above generally require major commitments over the long-term. They may require bold steps – with the related issue that they may be difficult or risky to implement in practice. For example, consider the position of Air Liquide – a major producer and distributor of industrial gases such as oxygen, nitrogen, helium and argon. It might want to become the global leader in its industry – allowing it to achieve economies of scale in technology and investment costs – but in practice how does it build share in markets where there are already established competitors?

One approach is to seek inspiration from the strategies used by companies that have built share against entrenched competition. One such example is *building a beachhead* in a new market before moving on. The Japanese motorbike manufacturers, having failed to sell many of their bigger bikes, switched to selling smaller

163

ones – later using the same platform built to go up market. Air Liquide might start by building a single plant for a large customer, using that to expand its presence gradually. Another example is *judo strategy* – in which you work around, or even use the strength of an incumbent against them. For example, a new entrant such as Aire Liquide may be able to under price established incumbents initially to build scale, because the incumbent is loath to respond, as it will damage its profitable business. Another approach, suggested by Clayton Christensen, is to be a disruptive competitor, as discussed in Chapter 4 – perhaps selling gases with lower purity at lower prices to carve out a niche that the incumbent is loath to compete in, because it will undermine their profitable core business.

Books and articles on strategy will contain other examples of successful strategies. The more you read, the more examples you can collect. Be warned, however: not all strategies should or will fit these simplistic models. At a minimum you need to select examples that are relevant to your industry and situation.

GENERATING OPTIONS THAT DEAL WITH UNCERTAINTY

It is particularly important to spend time generating a broad range of options when there is a high degree of uncertainty. A common trap is to focus on options that will be successful in one particular future. These options may look good on paper, but be vulnerable if the world turns out differently to what was expected.

There are no foolproof ways to generate good options under such difficult conditions, but here are a few ideas to get you going:

▶ Think of options that are robust under as many future scenarios as possible. For example, E.ON, the German power generation company, is investing in a mix of nuclear power, fossil fuels and renewable energies.

▶ Now think of one or more events not captured in the scenarios but which are credible – for example the risk that power demand falls because many households install their own small-scale power plants. Then, think of additional options that would allow you to profit from such a change, for example, investing in an energy services business that was well positioned to install and maintain such equipment.

▶ Think of options that provide agility and flexibility, so that you can seize options or respond to potential threats. For example, consider options that minimise fixed costs and capital investment – for example by signing contracts for 10% of your predicted power needs with other generators, including terms that allow you to cancel the contracts under certain conditions.

▶ Devise options that are robust and resilient to your worst case environment. For example, during a boom it may be good to build up cash so that you can buy assets and competitors during the bust, when prices are low.

▶ Develop options that allow you to learn as you go. Small investments, even if not attractive in themselves, may provide a platform for learning and getting access to more lucrative opportunities. For example, Apple's joint venture with Motorola to create the unsuccessful Moto phone in the mid-2000s allowed it to learn about making phones – knowledge which it put to good use when developing the iPhone.

WHO SAID IT . . .

". . . companies have to be very schizophrenic. On one hand, they have to maintain continuity of strategy. But they also have to be good at continuously improving."
– Michael Porter

GENERATING CUNNING OPTIONS

The best strategy options are often difficult to identify. The more obvious ones may be too incremental, too risky, or too costly. It often takes a flash of insight to generate the cunning option which is only obvious with the benefit of hindsight.

For example, when Unilever announced its new, improved Persil Power detergent, what strategy should P&G (Proctor and Gamble – Unilever's primary competitor) have used to defend its market share? The classic response would have been to increase promotional spend and look to launch its own improved product. In fact, P&G released a study suggesting that repeated washing with the new Unilever product put holes in boxer shorts. Unilever denied the allegations but changed the product formulation anyway. The battle dragged on and eventually Unilever conceded that the 'miracle' manganese compound did indeed attack certain dyes under extreme conditions, and withdrew it from the market.

Cunning options are of most value when you are in a tight spot – as P&G appeared to be when Unilever launched its new product. By defining the issue you face in unusual ways (in the case of P&G this was 'How do we undermine Unilever's product advantage'), then you may be able to generate creative options by considering how other organisations dealt with similar situations. It

WHO YOU NEED TO KNOW
Edward de Bono

Edward de Bono was born in Malta in 1933. He holds degrees in medicine and psychology, but most people round the world associate him with 'lateral thinking' – a term he invented. He contrasts what he calls 'vertical thinking', which uses the processes of logic, with its 'lateral' alternative, which 'involves thinking in new ways that generate new options and ideas'.

His skill has been to bring his thinking and methods to a wide audience (ranging from 7 year-olds to CEOs), suggesting practical ways to improve the creativity of an individual or group. Particularly famous in this area is his idea of 'six hats' – roles that six different members of a group can play to maximise the chance of generating new ideas. Another of his creativity tools is 'the power of perception' – which emphasises the benefits of looking at a problem from different angles, allowing the situation to be framed and analysed properly.

De Bono's work stands as a reminder of the fact that humans are, by nature, both dogmatic and limited in our vision and yet capable of occasional great leaps of insight. It also reminds us how hard it is to think outside the box.

is hard to create a comprehensive list of problems that need cunning solutions as – by definition – they tend to be unique. However, here are a few of the more typical examples:

▶ *Dealing with a threat.* The ideal strategy is to turn the threat into an opportunity – as P&G did by making the new Persil a millstone around Unilever's neck.

► *Taking on a dominant competitor* as in the case of the Japanese motorbike manufacturers entering the US and UK.

► *Creating a market for a new product* as in the case of the Nordic mobile phone manufacturers and operators – who created a single network that gave customers a service in all four countries as early as 1981 (unlike in the US – which had a much slower start because each network developed independently).

► *Breaking compromises.* A product requiring a mix of high-quality engineering, style and low cost might be seen as requiring tradeoffs and compromises – but this is what Swatch created when it came up with its innovative range of watches.

► *Overcoming organisational or cultural resistance.* For example, the inventor of Post-it notes got senior management interested in his product by giving samples to their personal assistants. When their bosses saw them they asked for more supplies.

Other factors which may inspire a cunning option include luck, persistence and a creative strategy process or the use of creativity tools such as those promoted by Edward de Bono. Whichever you use, leave yourself enough time; you are unlikely to find a solution quickly. Indeed, you may require several attempts before any such option reveals itself.

Before moving to discussing how to evaluate all these options it is worth summarising briefly the various approaches to generating options discussed so far – if only because the list of alternative approaches may seem overwhelming.

To *increase* the range of options you can try reframing the problem by brainstorming, or by considering different combinations of objectives and constraints. To test whether you have the right objectives you can use the '5 Whys' tool.

There are many ways to generate new options directly, including brainstorming, thinking of the options implied by different combinations of reasonable objectives and feasible pathways, using the strategy tools introduced earlier, considering generic strategies, spending extra time on considering options designed to work in a particularly uncertain future and pushing for cunning options based on the examples of others in a similar position.

If you are worried that you are spreading your resources too thin you may want to *reduce* the range of options and an effective way of doing so is to narrow the frame. Similar techniques can be applied to those discussed earlier – just ensure that your narrow frame is consistent with the overall strategic objective and mission, and feasible given the available pathways.

EVALUATING OPTIONS

All the good work to date will come to nought if you do not select the best option. Your options can be evaluated using three types of criteria: strategic, feasibility and risk/return.

Strategic criteria reflect the main strategy concepts introduced in this book, such as segmentation, segment attractiveness and competitive advantage. The figure below provides a checklist to structure this evaluation – each criterion is scored using 'traffic lights' (red, amber or green) depending on how it rates. A rule of thumb is that even a single red would be enough to prompt serious concerns about a strategy; at a minimum, a plan to tackle the issue would be required. One or two greens, in important categories, would be required for the strategy to be attractive.

Given the broad mix of potential strategies and organisations to which these traffic lights might be applied, it's impossible to be more precise about what constitutes an acceptable mix of reds, ambers and greens. For example, the issue of competitive advantage is often the dominant criterion in a competitive industry, but competitive advantage may be less relevant for a defence company that enjoys a quasi monopoly position vis-à-vis the national government. In such a case it may be more important to create value for the primary customer, thus ensuring maintenance of the favoured relationship. So a first step

OPTIONS EVALUATION CHECKLIST

1. Does the option position the organisation in large, growing industry segments?
   - ☐ Red light: Small or declining
   - ☐ Amber light: Average growth and size
   - ☐ Green light: Very large or high growth
2. Does the option position the organisation in profitable industry segments?
   - ☐ Red light: Particularly low profitability industry with low returns for even well established players
   - ☐ Amber light: Average industry returns
   - ☐ Green light: Exceptionally profitable industry or niche
3. Is the option aligned with the broader trends that are shaping the industry?
   - ☐ Red light: Option will require confronting significant external political, government or regulatory interference
   - ☐ Amber light: Broader trends have limited impact on the outcome of the options
   - ☐ Green light: Broader trends could provide significant support and upside for the option
4. Does the strategy create significant value for customers and stakeholders?
   - ☐ Red light: Option will destroy value for customers and stakeholders
   - ☐ Amber light: Limited impact on value creation
   - ☐ Green light: Options offers opportunities for significant new value generation
5. Will the option provide a competitive advantage, including any additional advantage that comes from linkages across segments?
   - ☐ Red light: Disadvantaged
   - ☐ Amber light: Me-too player
   - ☐ Green light: Significant, sustainable advantage

6. Is the option aligned with the mission, purpose, values and behaviours of the organisation?
   - ☐ Red light: Significant challenge to deeply held beliefs and behaviours
   - ☐ Amber light: Option is consistent
   - ☐ Green light: Option makes a significant contribution to purpose

7. Is the option aligned with the interests of the most influential stakeholders?
   - ☐ Red light: Powerful stakeholders will strongly resist
   - ☐ Amber light: Effects will be broadly neutral
   - ☐ Green light: Option is aligned to the interests of the most powerful stakeholders

8. Is the strategy adaptive and/or resilient to the type of uncertainties that might be faced?
   - ☐ Red light: Significant uncertainty exists and option will only be successful under a limited range of future scenarios
   - ☐ Amber light: Some flexibility to respond to known and unknown uncertainties
   - ☐ Green light: Option will result in a competitive advantage from being more flexible or resilient than others

9. Does the strategy allow the organisation the ability to create strategic options for the future?
   - ☐ Red light: Highly valuable capabilities or options are lost
   - ☐ Amber light: Some future options closed off, but others remain
   - ☐ Green light: Significant option value from options or capabilities created

10. Is the analysis based on a robust understanding of the evolving external and internal environment, and the full range of options?
    - ☐ Red light: Suspect data and insights
    - ☐ Amber light: Further analysis of key assumptions possible
    - ☐ Green light: Thoroughly analysed

in using the traffic lights should be to prioritise them according to your situation. It may also be necessary to add some particularly important criteria, like a particularly important source of competitive advantage.

WHO SAID IT . . .

"There are two things to be considered with regard to any scheme. In the first place, 'Is it good in itself?' In the second, 'Can it be easily put into practice?'."
– Jean Jacques Rousseau

EVALUATING FEASIBILITY

The traffic lights will help establish whether an option is a good one in principle. However, it is also important to double check whether it is feasible and can be implemented in practice. Criteria typically vary according to the situation, but might include:

- ▶ Are the required resources and capabilities available?
- ▶ Is the management team up to the job?

▶ Is there a strong sponsor?

▶ Will it be acceptable to key stakeholders?

▶ Is the option likely to have significant negative side effects and thus face resistance from other parts of the organisation?

▶ Are there suitable suppliers and partners to allow us to operate?

There may also be criteria specific to the context. For example, in acquiring a new business, a critical issue would be 'Can we manage the post-merger integration?' In entering a new country, there may be issues such as 'Can we get the required permits to operate?'

Just because these criteria are listed at the end of the analysis does not mean that you should wait until late in the strategy process to think about them. Thinking about feasibility should start during the evaluation of the external and internal environments – well before you get to this point. Otherwise you are in danger of committing one of the cardinal sins of strategy: devising an un-implementable strategy.

EVALUATING RISK/RETURN

When both strategy and feasibility criteria have been applied, it is common to summarise the assessment by comparing the potential return with the risks. There will be a mix of options that might be acceptable, each with a different combination of risk and return (obviously, you can reject options that have lower return for the same risk).

Measures of *return* are often set partly by the financial policies of the organisation and will include metrics such as profitability, payback or discounted payback, net present value and return on investment.

There are many ways of measuring and analysing *risk*. The most common, in order of sophistication, include:

▶ *Listing the main risks.* By simply describing the risks it is possible to get a better gut feel about the level and nature of the risks involved in different options.
▶ *Sensitivity analysis.* This involves measuring the potential impact of the risks on operating and financial metrics, such as time to market, investment cost, margins and payback.
▶ *Base, upside and downside cases.* This uses the results from the sensitivity analysis to build a set of possible scenarios for how the strategy may turn out, measuring the financial performance of each.
▶ *Probability trees.* This involves assigning probabilities to the base, upside and downside cases to get a more precise measure of the impact of risk on the expected performance of the strategy.
▶ *More detailed analysis of specific risks.* For complex and major risks, special modelling might

be required – for example, the impact of foreign exchange rate fluctuations on an investment in a manufacturing plant that imports
and exports components, or the impact of
changes in fuel prices and demand on the
prices for power enjoyed by a new gas-fired
power station.

The numbers can be vital for prioritising which risks to
worry about and their potential impact, but don't assume
that they will do all the thinking for you. Strategic decisions are typically helped by the development of some
well-grounded facts and numbers, but rarely can they be
mechanically answered this way. There are likely to be
some issues which cannot be quantified in the risk/
return analysis.

TIP: To help you weigh the pros and cons of different
options, a good discipline is to create a simple table of
the most attractive options arrayed against the most
important strategic, implementation and risk/return criteria. Not only is this a useful check on your logic, it
provides a great basis for discussion.

ITERATING

The most important point to remember from this chapter
can be stated quite simply: Make sure you go round the
cycle of framing the issue, generating and evaluating

options several times! The process has been described in a sequential way. However, it is almost always the case that it is an iterative, cyclical affair – as is often the case for the whole strategy process. As you analyse the situation and how it may evolve, you will begin to frame the issue and come up with options. As you evaluate the options, they may prove to be less appealing than you had hoped, prompting more analysis and a reframing of the question until new options emerge. This may happen in an orderly way but it is more likely you will encounter a lot of confusing ideas and distractions that you will need to pick your way through.

To illustrate, President Kennedy initially framed the Cuban missile crisis, in which the US unexpectedly discovered that the Soviets were putting nuclear missiles into Cuba, as 'How do we get those missiles out of Cuba?', receiving a range of military options in response. As his team explored the risks of nuclear war that such options entailed, they re-framed the question: 'How do we get the Russians to withdraw the missiles?' – eventually yielding the option of putting a blockade in place, which ultimately brought the Russians to the negotiating table.

Sometimes the process of framing and reframing can take years. For example, Steve Jobs had framed the idea of getting Apple into the music business in 2001 or earlier, but the iTunes store was not launched until 2003. The framing, and the options evolved over that period from 'How to get into the music business', to 'How to make music available on the Macintosh computer', to 'What music player to develop', to 'How to get the music industry to give Apple the rights to sell their music over the net.'

So how can you best navigate through this process? First, like checking your answers at the end of an exam, it makes sense to spend some time revisiting the framing of the issue and your chosen option. You may be exhausted at the end of a long strategy process, but don't rush things at the end. Put your work away for a day or two, refresh yourselves if you can, and then come back and tear it apart to see if the logic is robust.

The key to making this work is to imagine new frames and/or new options. Be prepared to introduce new people and perspectives as late on in the strategy process as you dare. Try packaging your logic using the Pyramid Principle to highlight any weaknesses. Ask yourself the question: 'But what if we have framed this in the wrong way – what is another way to do it?' Build in the ability to learn and respond as the strategy evolves.

WHAT YOU NEED TO READ

▶ Zook's trilogy on growth consists of *Profit from the Core*, *Beyond the Core*, and *Unstoppable*, Harvard Business School Press, 2001, 2003 and 2007.

▶ The '5 Whys' technique, developed initially at Toyota, is discussed at *http://en.wikipedia.org/wiki/5_Whys*.

▶ The 'Who What How' analysis was first proposed by Derek Abell and developed further by Costas Markides in 'All the Right Moves', *Harvard Business School Press*, 2000 and in his article 'Six Principles of Breakthrough Strategy' in *Business Strategy Review*, 1999, Volume 10, Issue 2 pages 1-10. There are various variants involving deconstruction of these three dimensions, e.g. 'Who' into 'Customer', 'Need' and 'Channel'.

▶ *De Bono's Thinking Course: Powerful Tools to Transform Your Thinking*, BBC Active, 2006 provides a summary of much of his thinking.

▶ *Profiting from Uncertainty: Strategies for Succeeding No Matter What the Future Brings*, The Free

Press, 2002, by Paul J.H. Schoemaker provides many ideas about how to create strategy under uncertainty.

▶ Chapters 3 and 4 of 'Harvard Business Essentials: Strategy', *Harvard Business School Press*, 2005, provide several examples of generic strategies.

▶ *Strategy: How to Shape the Future of the Business*, Format Publishing, 2004, edited by Dominic Houlder, is a stimulating read and provides interesting ideas on collaborative strategies.

IF YOU ONLY REMEMBER ONE THING

Reframe and iterate at least three times!

CHAPTER 6
THE PRIORITIES

WHAT IT'S ALL ABOUT

► Approaches to sequencing the strategy questions

► The pros and cons of different approaches

► How to choose the right approach

You now have the concepts and tools to come up with a strategy. But, a survey of how this is done in practice would suggest that there is no one single way in which strategy is developed. It can be created by the corporate CEO, or it can involve many individuals across the organisation. It can be a big, one-off exercise, or evolve as a series of smaller decisions taken over time. It can involve cumulative adjustments to a well-known business, or big bets in areas fraught with uncertainty. It can be made by careful analysts using a highly structured process or by highly intuitive individuals, who would find such structure frustrating. Strategy processes do not follow standard norms. How do you pick a sensible approach?

A good place to start is by considering which of the strategy questions should be your priority. One approach is to give equal weight to each question, going through each in turn (sometimes called the 'planning', 'analytical' or 'positioning' approach). At the opposite extreme you can do no analysis at all but simply try something, learn from the results, and adjust accordingly (sometimes called the 'learning', 'emergent' or 'incremental' approach). Between these is a spectrum of approaches which seek to capture the benefits of the two extremes. For example, you can skip questions where you are confident that you already know the answer. You can go through the questions in a 'quick and dirty' fashion, and circle back later to spend more time on those questions where you feel unsure.

The full range of common approaches, and how you select the right one for your situation, is the topic of this chapter. In parallel, you will need to think about who should be involved and in what kind of process – issues which will be addressed in following chapters.

THE FULL MONTY APPROACH

The most obvious sequence is to follow the cogs through one by one (see the following diagram, which also includes some sub-questions that a 'Full Monty' approach might cover). This is typically used when investigating a relatively new situation where there is a high level of uncertainty about the options and it is important to get the right answer. A typical Full Monty strategy study might involve a team of four people analysing the first three cogs for six to eight weeks, investigating customer needs, market trends, the general industry context, competitors and the economics of the business. This would culminate in an assessment of the current situation and future trends, and a summary of the main issues, together with an initial view of the options. The next phase, which might take two to four weeks, would flesh out and evaluate the options. The final stage would create an implementation plan, leading to the roll-out of the new strategy.

The weakness of this approach is that it is costly and takes a long time. One way round this is to prioritise the

Basic questions in strategy

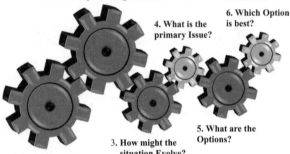

2. What is the Internal situation?
- What are our objectives?
- What value are we creating for customers?
- What is our competitive advantage?
- How are we performing?

4. What is the primary Issue?

6. Which Option is best?

5. What are the Options?

3. How might the situation Evolve?
- What are the key uncertainties?
- How might they evolve?
- Which are the most important?

1. What is the External environment?
- What industry segments are we in?
- How attractive are those segments?
- What is the influence of the macro environment?

analysis, focusing your time on one particular question or sub-question.

To illustrate, the management team of a competitor to Hewlett Packard in laser printers identified that the main area where HP out-compated them was in the user-friendly design of the printers and printer software. To address this issue, they carried out a focused study to answer just one question: 'What is HP's product development process for their laser printer?' The project provided insights that addressed the main weakness of the company and avoided the need for a full analysis of customers, markets, competitors, etc.

The Full Monty is, therefore, a last resort to be used when you are highly uncertain about most aspects of the situation – for example, if you are entering into a new country or new market, or are concerned that false assumptions are being made about the current strategy.

WHO YOU NEED TO KNOW
Kenneth Andrews

Kenneth Andrews (1916–2005) began as an authority on Mark Twain and ended up as a professor at Harvard Business School and one of most influential early thinkers in the area of corporate leadership and strategy.

Andrews completed his PhD at HBS in 1948 and shortly afterwards became part of a group looking at the structure of Harvard's Business Policy course – which was designed to present students with the problems of an entire organisation from the perspective of its leader. Eventually, the core concept developed by this group was termed 'corporate strategy'. Fundamental to his approach was 'SWOT analysis' – the idea that an organisation's direction should be determined by its strengths, weaknesses, opportunities and threats.

Andrews believed that strategy should lead to purposeful action. His view was that 'every business organization, every subunit of organization, and even every individual [ought to] have a clearly defined set of purposes or goals which keeps it moving in a *deliberately chosen direction* and prevents its drifting in undesired directions' (emphasis added). He also developed the idea that the long-term success of the organisation required a distinctive competence – in many ways a foundation for later theories of competitive advantage.

Andrews' work is no longer widely read.
Some of it seems out of date in a world of
rapid technological change, global competition,
and organisations that lack the command-
and-control structures of the era he lived in.
Nevertheless, he is a key player in the
emergence of business strategy thinking
from the post-war US economy and academic
establishment, particularly that at Harvard
Business School.

THE QUICK-AND-DIRTY APPROACH

Decision makers often use their intuition and experience
to move rapidly to initial hypotheses or even conclusions.
They skip through the questions, answering as best and
as quickly as they can, circling back to do more detailed
work as needed. Using this 'quick-and-dirty' approach
allows them to rapidly pinpoint any obvious options
that do not require further analysis or consideration but
can be implemented immediately. More generally, the

quick-and-dirty approach will indicate what strategy questions need more follow-up.

For example, when the Malaysian government was looking for ways to industrialise by adding more value to the natural rubber that they produced, a quick-and-dirty review led them to realise that tyres were one of the biggest markets for rubber, but that this was a large, global and competitive business. They then commissioned a detailed study into options that would allow Malaysia to compete against the major global competitors in Japan, Korea, the US and Europe. The quick-and-dirty approach thus generated some initial hypotheses which they were able to develop and test with a more detailed study.

WHO SAID IT . . .

"We don't have a traditional strategy process, planning process like you'd find in traditional technical companies. It allows Google to innovate very, very quickly, which I think is a real strength of the company."
– **Eric Schmidt**

The strength of the quick-and-dirty approach is that it enables rapid focus of the work effort by identifying what is known and where more work needs to be done. As a result, it is a very common approach and generally a good one.

The one risk is that prejudices and misleading assumptions can be baked into the strategy early on. There is a danger that any strategy work will focus primarily on proving the initial hypotheses rather than being open to contradictory data. It is sometimes beneficial to allow time to simply collect data and reflect on what they might imply. If this risk can be guarded against – for example, by exposing the initial output to sceptical opinion – the quick-and-dirty approach can be a useful precursor to more detailed strategy work.

The 'quick-and-dirty with follow-up' approach may result in a decision to go through a Full Monty, or it may confirm that enough is already known to permit a more focused and efficient approach. We now describe common versions of these more focused approaches.

THE FUTURE THINKING APPROACH

This starts by focusing not on the current situation but on the third question: 'How might the situation evolve?' Thus the strategy process begins with the creation of scenarios of how the future might take shape. A number of credible alternative futures are created and the position of the organisation under each scenario is evaluated. Organisations also commonly conduct thought experiments or studies into how they would perform if the economy unexpectedly contracted or expanded.

WHO SAID IT . . .

". . . whereas all experiences are of the past, all decisions are about the future. The image of the future, therefore, is the key to all choice-oriented behaviour."
— Kenneth Boulding

This approach is useful for organisations in environments undergoing rapid change. For example, a consumer products company such as Sony might consider how consumer lifestyles and technology are changing in order to identify new markets to target; a car company might think about how technologies such as electronic controls or batteries will develop and the effect on the automotive business.

Another time to use 'future thinking' is when the organisation needs to be kick-started into thinking more creatively. It is said that if you drop a frog into a pan of hot water it will leap out, but that if you put it in cold water and heat it up slowly, the frog will stay in the pan until it is cooked. It is not possible to vouch for the validity of the science (no scientist has admitted trying out the experiment since it was performed in the nineteenth century), but the analogy is that the human brain tends to be poor at reacting to changes that occur incrementally. Sometimes, people need to be shocked into realising that the strategic temperature is rising and that they must come up with creative options.

This approach was used in South Africa in the apartheid era to bring black and white leaders together. The scenario-planning function at Anglo American, the mining multinational, put together a presentation envisioning two scenarios for South Africa: the 'high road' of negotiation, leading to a political settlement, and the 'low road' of confrontation leading to civil war, and used it to influence the thinking of both the Afrikaner and ANC camps. It was in part as a result of this that South Africa ultimately took the high road.

Shell famously used scenarios of the future oil business to sensitise their 1970s senior management team to what might happen if oil prices rose significantly. When this actually transpired, Shell reacted more quickly than its competitors.

These examples illustrate the power of addressing the question 'How might the situation evolve?' It forces people to challenge their own assumptions about the situation and how it might develop, and to arrive at more innovative and powerful options than they would otherwise envisage.

To start with this question requires that the participants in the strategy process already have extensive knowledge of the current situation, to be able to build credible future scenarios rather than fantasies. For this reason, the exercise is often done as a team – because only a team will have enough breadth of experience to develop a set of broad-ranging scenarios. For example, if Apple wanted to think about how the market for hand-held devices will develop, it might put together a group that includes a technology specialist, an expert on customer needs, someone who understands what its competitors are doing, and an expert on the likely development of relevant markets such as MP3 players, PDAs and mobile phones.

THE ISSUES APPROACH

If you are knowledgeable about the current situation *and* how it may evolve, it can be efficient to use the 'Frame the Issue' approach and jump straight in with the fourth question: 'What is the primary issue?' Doing so will create a discussion about the nature of the issue and the available options to deal with it.

Consider the example of a regional power distribution company that owned and operated the power lines that bring power from the national high-voltage grid to homes and businesses, which was struggling to meet its profit targets. Different members of the management team saw the issues facing the business in different ways. For some, the issue was 'How do we cut costs to maintain and grow profits?' This framing led to various options for improving operational effectiveness, for example, through improvements in working practices. For others, the issue was 'How do we compete as a small competitor in a business with much larger competitors?' For this group, the options were to do with the choice of acquisition targets and ways to improve economies of scale by outsourcing some activities to larger companies. A third group saw the issue as 'How do we find new sources of profitable growth?' This framing implied a search for new business, such as the installation and operation of solar panels and the provision of extra services to larger customers. The discussion of these different ways to frame the issue led to a rich range of options, all of which could then be analysed in more detail.

As with 'future thinking', this approach can rapidly open up minds to new possibilities. It generates very different ideas about what is the most important strategic issue, and thus what options should be considered further. For experienced managers, it enables them to rapidly share ideas, identify differences of opinion and agree on a list of topics for further analysis.

However, it requires that the team understand enough about the current situation and how it might develop to be able to sensibly frame the issue. There is a risk that framing the issue too early may result in too narrow a range of options being addressed, so it can be helpful to come back later and revisit the nature of the issue. With the benefit of more information, the team may realise that they are addressing the wrong issue and need to reframe their view.

THE OPTIONS APPROACH

An experienced decision maker will often use the question, 'What are the options?', to cut to the chase – even right at the beginning of the strategy process. It can be done by asking each person to state their favoured option or by asking the group to list all possible options. This focuses any further data gathering, analysis and debate on those activities required to make the choice from this list.

This approach is similar to framing the issue but some find it more practical to discuss alternative options rather than alternative definitions of the issue. For example, an alternative approach for the power distribution company would have been to ask every team member to list all the options that they thought should be considered. Given the mix of views within the management team, this would have revealed a wide range of options – ranging from negotiations with the unions over working practices, to entering new businesses such as solar panels. This would in turn have led to a process of prioritising and evaluating the options in more detail.

Another advantage of thinking about options is that it counterbalances the potential effect of anchoring on a particular option. One problem with relying on a sequential 'Full Monty' process, starting with an analysis of the situation, is that team members may start forming their own views about the best options as the analysis progresses (as we will see later, it is human nature to jump to conclusions). By the time the process arrives at the question 'What are the options?' they already have a favourite rooted in their mind. Starting with a discussion about different options can ensure that a wider range is generated before personal or group biases take hold.

A good discussion about options requires that the decision-making team has a sound understanding of the answers to the previous questions in the strategy sequence. It is no good starting with a discussion of options if you are not familiar with the external and internal situation, how it is likely to develop, and the strategic issues that need to be addressed.

WHO YOU NEED TO KNOW
Henry Mintzberg

Henry Mintzberg, (b. 1939) is a prolific writer on strategy, management and organisation. Since 1968 he has been a professor at McGill University in Montreal. In the area of strategy, one of his main contributions has been to point out, and critique, the many ways in which strategy is *actually* created, rather than how (according to certain other writers) it *should* be created. Mintzberg is a vigorous critic of formal 'strategy planning' – a coupling that he views as an oxymoron.

The habit of pointing out misconceptions about management started with his PhD, looking at what five CEOs actually spent their time doing. This led to a book published in 1973 called 'The Nature of Managerial Work', debunking the idea that managers spend their time creating plans and controlling their execution.

He turned his attention to strategy making in the 1990s, pointing out that strategy is not simply planned – it often 'emerges' as a result of chance, small decisions and opportunism. He further developed a critique of strategy formulation, and in '*Strategy Safari*' summarised several ways in which the process of strategy creation has been described. He advocates a more holistic view of the different ways in which strategy can be created.

Mintzberg is much more than just a gadfly – although to many of his victims he certainly plays that role. He is also a serious academic who has fought to ensure that management thinking is humanised and useful. Even those who believe that he sometimes oversells his point, acknowledge that he does at least make a vigorous defence of his case.

Any serious student of strategy must read some Mintzberg, even if only as an antidote to some of the rather dreary writing in this field. Mintzberg is a gifted synthesizer, writer and speaker and has written excellent books on strategy formation, organisational structure, power, management and management education.

THE TEST-AND-LEARN APPROACH

A rather different approach is to answer the questions not by thinking about possible answers but by trying something to see if it works. The supermarket chain Tesco, for example, spends little time worrying how customers will respond to a particular new grocery product; it simply tries selling it. If it sells, it may tweak the offer to see if that works better; if it doesn't sell, it will think of another experiment. The cumulative effect of these multiple small experiments is that its strategy in groceries will evolve into something different and more effective.

This test-and-learn approach (also described as 'Ready, Fire, Aim') can be very powerful, particularly in markets where there is no seismic shift required but plenty of small, incremental uncertainties about customer needs, competitive actions and market development. Tesco's rivals have found that even if they launch a new product successfully, Tesco will copy it and roll it out quicker than they could in their own stores.

Unfortunately, some organisations do the 'test' without the 'learn'. Many managers are superb 'do-ers' – good at mobilising the troops, promoting the product or ramping up production. They reach a decision and act but then do not learn from the results, because the organisation is not set up to record and act upon them. To add the capability to learn generally takes a major investment. It took Tesco years to build the required IT systems and train up its employees to feed in the data correctly and then use it. In a different industry, professional services firms invest extensively in knowledge management systems and organisational processes that encourage the recording and sharing of knowledge – a process that also takes several years to mature and, if the culture does not encourage sharing, may never deliver the benefits it promises.

Investing in test-and-learn does not come cheap. Moreover, while it is great at creating evolutionary change it is unlikely to uncover radically new solutions. (By way of an analogy, amphibians evolved by increments into reptiles and reptiles into birds, but they didn't suddenly transform into trees or mammals). For this reason, Tesco has a strategy function to reflect upon major changes that the test-and-learn approach cannot deal with, for example, entering new countries or new businesses such as pharmacies or financial services. Most test-and-learn strategies need to be complemented by some of the other approaches to creating strategy described earlier.

ONE MORE APPROACH: INTUITIVE BOUNCING

Most of the approaches described so far start with one particular strategy question and use it to identify further work to be done. An alternative is to bounce intuitively from one strategy question to another. For teams who are used to discussing strategy this is a free-wheeling technique that can be efficient in terms of time, exchanging ideas and getting to the heart of the issue.

This approach can be very effective – indeed it's the one that an expert team would most naturally use – particularly in a fast-moving environment where strategy needs to be frequently discussed and refined. However, the danger is that it can descend into chaos, leaving key uncertainties unaddressed and allowing personal biases to drive the decision. It also requires the team to be steeped in the required information (although knowledge can be split across different members of the group), trust each other and work well together.

Leave time in your strategy-making for bouncing. Create opportunities to meet and brainstorm around the questions in an unstructured way. But don't forget to regroup and restructure the work effort at the end of your meeting.

HOW TO PICK THE RIGHT APPROACH

There are many ways to prioritise the questions. How do you pick the right one? The following chart draws up the alternative approaches, summarising their respective pros and cons.

To choose the right approach for your specific situation, first review the strategy questions and ask which ones you

Alternative ways to sequence the questions

Approach	Description	Pros	Issues/comments
The Full Monty	• Start with "What is the current situation" • Ensure rigorous and logical answers to all questions before proceeding to next one	• Rigorous • Builds solid fact base on which options and decisions are securely founded	• Slow • Expensive
Quick and Dirty, with Follow Up	• Quick run through all questions, then focus on questions/sub-questions requiring more attention	• Allows quick sharing of ideas • Identifies areas requiring further analysis and debate	• Requires reasonable knowledge and/or diversity of opinion to avoid jumping to conclusions prematurely
Future thinking	• Start with "How might the situation develop?" – then draw out issues, options, further analysis required	• Stimulates creativity about the current situation, issues and options	• Requires good prior knowledge of the current situation
Frame the issue	• Start with "What is the primary issue?" – then identify options/ further analysis required	• Allows rapid focus on most relevant options • Stimulates discussion of alternative frames	• Requires good prior knowledge of current situation and how it is likely to develop
What are the options	• Start with "What are the options?" – then identify further analysis required	• Mostdirect approach • Stimulates discussion of alternatives	• Requires sound understanding of answers to prior questions
Test and learn	• Try something – adjust strategy based on results	• Effective when many small uncertainties	• May result in evolutionary changes only
Intuitive bouncing	• Jump between questions, punctuated by periods of focus on critical questions	• Permits focus on most important questions	• Can descend into chaos • Requires experienced strategists

think you have a good answer to. Ideally, do this with a group to make sure you get a relatively unbiased view. It may help to use the quick-and-dirty approach to find out where there is agreement, where there is disagreement, and where there is simply ignorance.

Interview some of the key individuals and experts to flesh out what they think are the main issues and options, their views about the external and internal environments, and how they will evolve. During these early discussions, be curious, listen well and probe carefully. Look out for differences in the key assumptions on which individuals are basing their world view, as such conflicts often indicate where the strategy process should focus.

A useful technique for getting to the root of such assumptions is the '5 Whys' described in the previous chapter. Ask the individual who has made a broad statement why they believe it. This will reveal an underlying assumption. Then ask why that assumption is held. Continue until you understand all the underlying assumptions on which an individual is basing their view.

It may be helpful to create a 'fact pack' that summarises the relevant information that is already available. Ask others to contribute to the fact pack to avoid doing unnecessary data collection and analysis.

If, after this process, you are confident that you have good answers to some of the early questions, you can start your strategy process by asking one of the later questions – using one of the four approaches that do so: Future thinking, Frame the issue, What are the options, or Test-and-learn. If not, you may need to settle for the Full Monty. Make sure you review the 'pros' column and the 'issues and comments' column in the table above before finalising your approach.

Don't allow limited time and resources to constrain the strategy process. It is better to get a bigger team or take more time than to come up with a flawed strategy. If you identify different viewpoints within the senior management team, this can be a powerful argument for insisting that you need to do the job properly.

As you develop the strategy, review your progress from time to time. You may need to come back to one of the earlier questions, such as 'What is the external environment?' to fill a critical gap in your knowledge or test a key assumption. Or you may realise that you are in a position to jump to the next question earlier than originally planned. Use the pyramid principle discussed in chapter one to test how your logic and storyline is developing. Ask an independent person or group to review and challenge your thinking. Be ready to change the questions you focus on, if needed.

The test and learn approach is a special case. It is only suitable when you have defined the broad strategy already (using one of the more analytical approaches), and when there is only a moderate, residual level of uncertainty. In such environments you can let the strategy evolve incrementally within a pre-defined envelope through the 'test and learn' approach. Be careful to check back occasionally to ensure that a more fundamental review is not required, as this approach is not effective at making step changes in direction.

You must be prepared for deviations from the proposed approach. For example, the 'intuitive bouncing' approach is useful in meetings or in situations where you have a very experienced team and need to make rapid decisions. Intuitive bouncing is part of the creative process – but don't let it cause the whole strategy process to slide into chaos.

WHAT YOU NEED TO READ

▶ The classic texts on the nature of the strategy process are *The Rise and Fall of Strategic Planning*, Prentice Hall, 1994 and its less academic version, *Strategy Safari*, FT Prentice Hall, 2002, both by Henry Mintzberg.

▶ A view of the strategy process in fast-moving industries, similar to the Quick and Dirty or Intuitive Bouncing approaches, is provided by Kathleen Eisenhardt in *Strategy as Strategic Decision Making* in the Sloan Management Review, Spring 1999, p. 65.

▶ Kenneth Andrews' classic, but very dated, book on strategy is *The Concept of Corporate Strategy*, Richard D Irwin, 1987.

▶ *Games Foxes Play*, Human & Rousseau and Tafelberg, 2005, by Chantell Ilbury and Clem Sunter provides a description of how to design a Future Thinking strategy process.

▶ Richard Koch's *The Financial Times Guide to Strategy* presents an example of the Full Monty approach and there is a more academic version in chapter 11 of *The Strategic Management of Organisations*, FT Prentice Hall, 2001 by Adrian Haberberg and Alison Rieple.

IF YOU ONLY REMEMBER ONE THING

Be thoughtful about which strategy questions to focus on, and in what order.

CHAPTER 7

PROCESS

WHAT IT'S ALL ABOUT

- Defining the ambition
- Dealing with uncertainty
- The fallible brain
- Improving objectivity with people and process
- Dealing with time pressures
- Creating a strategy team
- Spotting biases
- Fine-tuning the process

The previous chapter describes how to prioritise and sequence the strategy questions. This defines the skeleton – the broad characteristics – of the strategy process. For example, if you choose the Full Monty approach, you will need several weeks to collect and analyse data on the internal and external situation and on how things may trend over time. You must then spend time framing the issue and analysing your options. If, instead, you decide on the 'Options' approach, you might start by asking the management team about their preferred options, followed by a period spent analysing them, before ultimately presenting a choice to the team for discussion and approval. This process could, if necessary, be completed within a week.

Now it is time to add some flesh to the skeleton by answering the following questions about the process and the people to be involved:

- ▶ What should be the main activities? For example, data collection, analysis, brainstorming, engagement with the broader organisation, presentation preparation.
- ▶ What groups or teams do you need to involve? For example, project team, steering committee, advisory panel, the executive team, the board.
- ▶ Who should be in each group or team?
- ▶ How should the process be managed and facilitated?

▶ What should the timetable be?

▶ What review meetings are required?

▶ What is the decision-making and approval process?

It would be nice if there were best practices to apply, but strategy development must be customised to the situation. However, by answering the following questions you can come up with a reasonable design:

▶ What is the required ambition of the strategy?

▶ How precise should the strategy be?

▶ What are the main threats to objectivity?

▶ Who needs to be engaged?

DEFINING THE AMBITION

Strategy processes vary enormously depending on their ambition. Of particular importance are the *degree of change* and the *time frame* for the strategy.

At one extreme is the one-year planning cycle, in which the ambition is low. It involves no significant debate about strategy; it is essentially a process in which the detailed actions, plans and targets required to implement the current strategy are formalised. It is focused just on the short-term. Such a process will probably involve clarifying the strategic and financial targets, defining the actions required to achieve them, and creating a financial plan. It will involve the line management in each of the businesses and major departments, with reviews and approvals further up the hierarchy. The process may take weeks or even months and result in the formal approval of detailed targets, action plans and milestones. It will probably be repeated on an annual basis.

At the other extreme is a visioning exercise, imagining what the organisation might look like in the future. The ambition is high. Radical options need to be considered over a long time frame – perhaps 10 or 15 years.

Such a process will consist of very different activities to those of the one-year planning process. It might involve collecting ideas from the broader organisation and relevant stakeholders, extensive analysis of trends in the external environment, and a series of workshops with the executive team and the board. The process might be facilitated by a small team under the direct control of the chief executive – perhaps with the help of some external consultants.

To create an ambitious strategy will consume considerable management time and should only be undertaken when needed – for example when the current strategy is clearly no longer fit for purpose. How often this is depends on the company and the environment – but don't expect to be doing such an exercise very often.

PRECISION

The strategy process should reflect the level of detail required. This in turn will depend on the degree of uncertainty about the actions required to implement the strategy.

If there is little uncertainty, it is worth planning to a high level of detail as this will really 'pressure test' the strategy and assist its implementation. Those responsible for implementation will need to be heavily involved in the process, as will the finance function. Add time for the development of detailed plans and budgeting.

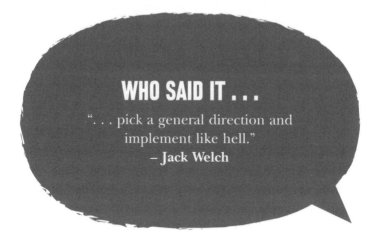

WHO SAID IT . . .

". . . pick a general direction and implement like hell."
– **Jack Welch**

On the other hand, if there is a high level of uncertainty, the strategy process simply needs to (in Jack Welch's words) set 'a general direction', allowing those responsible for implementation to adjust the strategy as the situation evolves. Greater emphasis on putting in place the capabilities and systems for learning and adaptation will be required. Less time will be needed on implementation planning, more on working out how the strategy is to be rolled out and adapted to the evolving situation – for example, by setting up a regular review of how implementation is progressing and giving different managers responsibility for monitoring the situation or trying out new approaches. There will be little point in doing a lot of detailed budgeting – for example, in the 2008 financial crisis some firms abandoned their traditional three or even one-year budgeting processes, choosing to budget quarter by quarter.

THE FALLIBLE BRAIN

The next question to consider is: What are the main threats to objectivity? Strategies are formed by a mix of individual and social decision making. Decisions are created not by spreadsheets, programmes and templates, but by the greatest computer in the world – the 100 billion neurons of the human brain. The quality of strategic decisions will be affected not just by the concepts and tools used, but how they are processed by the brain.

The way the brain makes decisions has been described by Herbert Simon, a Nobel prize-winning polymath, as 'boundedly rational' – it makes the best decision possible given the limitations on the data and processing power available to it, relying upon shortcuts and rules-of-thumb, known as heuristics, to come up with rational answers. Heuristics are constructed from past patterns and associations.

Normally this approach works pretty well. The human brain evolved over millions of years and generally makes good decisions. But it can get things wrong. Sometimes a decision based on patterns, associations and rules-of-thumb can get you into trouble. For an illustrative example, consider the following picture. What do you see?

What do you see?

What people observe depends on the area on which they focus. If they look at the lower left-hand side they see a set of black-topped stairs. If they look at the other side they see a cat sitting on a set of white-topped stairs.

How can the brain be so easily conned into accepting two incompatible points of view? The reason links back to the way that the brain interprets information according to past associations. It is used to the patterns in the image being a staircase, so it jumps to a conclusion that this is what it is seeing – adjusting its view of the orientation of the staircase according to which part of the picture it dwells on. It does not see the picture for what it is because it is not an object of which it has any experience or which it has evolved to recognise. The brain is not able to be *fully* rational and comprehend the contradictory nature of the image. Instead it is *boundedly* rational – it jumps to a conclusion within the bounds of its experience. Unfortunately, by doing so, it makes an incorrect decision.

Applying this notion to the world of business strategy, how many corporate acquirers have been highly successful, only to over-extend themselves and be brought down by one bad investment. For example, Guy Hands' Terra Firma group paid too much to acquire EMI, at a time when the music industry's profits were being eroded by the development of internet-based file-sharing. Hands stretched too far, assuming that he could do the same with EMI as he had done with other acquisitions. But past patterns proved to be a poor guide in this particular case. The aggressive management style for which he was renowned did not work well in a business reliant on building relationships with prima donnas, and led to many of EMI's star acts walking out.

Similarly, consider Rentokil's rapid demise when it over-stretched and acquired Securiguard and BET. These two large firms were in unfamiliar industries and could not easily be absorbed into Rentokil's business model, which was based on making many small acquisitions and integrating them into the Rentokil way of doing business. Rentokil's management team's experience was that acquisitions provided attractive opportunities for growth – leading them to underestimate the challenges of making a large acquisition in a new industry.

The brain is affected not only by embedded patterns and experience, but also by the personal interests and attachments of the decision maker. From Enron to MPs' expenses, examples abound of how people's decisions are distorted when their personal interests are involved. Perhaps Guy Hands was swayed by the idea of controlling a company with so many 'A-list' music stars – he is known to be a Meatloaf fan and is rumoured to have one of the world's largest collections of karaoke records.

The good news is that when answering strategy questions the brain tries to be objective; the bad news is that it may well fail. It can make snap decisions based on a partial

WHO YOU NEED TO KNOW
Daniel Kahneman

Daniel Kahneman is a Nobel Prize-winning psychologist based at Princeton University who, with his research partner Amos Tversky, established the field of behavioural economics, which posits that the 'rational being' previously assumed by the field of economics is a fiction. Rather, the brain makes decisions on the basis of cognitive, social and emotional factors. As a consequence, people's decisions are based on heuristics – rules-of-thumb that have worked reasonably well in the past. They frame events in ways which filter how they see the situation. This leads to a range of cognitive biases.

These ideas build on the work of Herbert Simon, who coined the terms 'bounded rationality' and 'satisficing' to describe the limits to human rationality.

Kahneman began his career in the psychology department of the Israeli Defence Forces, evaluating candidates for officer training school. He completed a PhD at Berkeley, California, returning to Israel where he began a 10-year collaboration with Tversky – who was denied the Nobel Prize himself by his untimely death, aged 59, in 1996. One of their most well-known papers is *Judgment Under Uncertainty: Heuristics and Biases*, which introduced the idea of 'anchoring'.

The field of behavioural economics has led to a wide-ranging and rapidly growing set of insights into the way people actually make decisions and how to improve the quality of those decisions – supported by insights from a range of other disciplines including neuroscience, evolutionary psychology, sociology and organisational studies.

knowledge of the external and internal situation. It can be over-confident about the degree to which it can predict the future. It may frame the primary issue incorrectly. It may not consider all the options or not apply all the necessary criteria when choosing an option.

Hence *a vital function of the strategy process is to increase the rationality and objectiveness of the decision* – and will be the subject of the rest of this chapter.

IMPROVING OBJECTIVITY WITH PROCESS AND PEOPLE

To improve objectivity, you should modify the strategy process to address any potential sources of irrational thinking. First, pinpoint areas where a lack of objectivity might creep in. Then consider adding appropriate process steps, experts, advisory bodies and more formal governance. Put in place the necessary meetings and reviews. Finally, define a decision process that provides adequate checks and balances.

Some typical weaknesses, and examples of what you can do to deal with them, are as follows:

Knowledge deficit. Where there is insufficient knowledge to make an objective decision – for example, if the strategy involves entering new markets or responding to a new competitor, you should allocate more time and resources to collecting information. This may require the support of a project team or outside experts for a lengthy period. If you are unsure about the nature of the investment required, first do some interviews to establish what you do and don't know.

If you are missing a lot of data it is sensible to organise the initial work around modules focused on generating 'fact packs' in critical areas. For example, you might have one person work on understanding customer needs, another laying out market trends, another doing analyses of competitors and a fourth looking at macro-trends. Then, when the data has been collected, you can re-focus the team on the strategy questions, making a summary of the external and internal environments and how they are likely to evolve. Another approach is to include people with different expertise – for example, by making the process more bottom-up or adding outsiders.

Challenge deficit. If there is too little disagreement and debate within the team, the risk is that you will zero-in on an answer too early. There are many ways to generate more challenge by changing the process. One is to force the decision maker to justify their argument and assumptions (the Minto Pyramid Principle can be useful for this). Another is to devote time to debating key assumptions and coming up with alternatives. For example, you can interview outsiders, ask everyone to write down their own ideas before starting a group debate, invite people to play contrarian roles, or appoint a leader whose primary role is to challenge assumptions.

Again, add people to the process who have different views and are prepared to defend them. They can either be part of the strategy team or used to create a steering committee. You can also use existing groups, such as the board, to provide challenge.

Consensus deficit. Conversely, there may be so much challenge that the strategy process becomes a feud between individuals or factions. It is important not to overreact to a heated debate – it may be exactly what your strategy process needs. But be aware of the tipping point at which healthy disagreements turn dysfunctional, endangering the strategy process and organisational harmony.

To reduce the risk of this happening, focus everyone on the goal – i.e. an objective strategy. Legitimise conflict and disagreement but establish ground rules that prevent arguments from becoming personal. Make sure that discussions are properly chaired. Consider changing the role or involvement of disruptive individuals, but without losing the benefits that mavericks, devil's advocates and contrarians can bring.

Ambition deficit. Even if you have defined the ambition, the strategy team may confine their approach to making small adjustments to the existing plan. If this is the case, apply some of the techniques in Chapter 5 for getting individuals to consider alternative frames and options. To reinforce this, challenge the team to think outside of their current boundaries and comfort zones, ensuring that the ambition is defined to include a suitably expansive review and design. Set stretching top down targets.

You can also add people able to think in a more radical or visionary way, although you may not want to draw them into the core of the process if, as a result, they lose their ability to think out of the box. A good steering committee or advisory panel can also help a team broaden its thinking.

Pragmatism deficit. The flipside of a lack of ambition is when there is no pragmatic concept of what is achievable in the short-term. To counteract this problem, increase the involvement of those responsible for implementing the strategy. Focus the group by asking them to come up with short-term actions that are both implementable and move the organisation towards its long-term vision.

Problems in coping with ambiguity and uncertainty. Sometimes those involved find it difficult to cope with the degree of uncertainty involved in making the decision. As a result, they may be overconfident about their ability to predict the future, or become paralysed in the face of so much uncertainty. This is a common phenomenon, particularly if they are used to dealing with more predictable, operational decisions.

One solution is to change the mix of people on your team. Another is to generate scenarios for the future to get people more comfortable with the level of uncertainty. (You can also use some of the other tools suggested in chapters 4 and 5). Continuously refer back to these scenarios to ensure that the strategy recognises the uncertainty about the way the future might evolve. Again, a good steering committee can help.

WHO YOU NEED TO KNOW
Jack Welch

Jack Welch, CEO of General Electric, is the most influential business leader of recent times. Born in 1935, Welch earned B.S., M.S. and PhD degrees in chemical engineering before joining GE and rising to become its eighth and youngest leader. Under his stewardship, the value of the firm rose from $13 billion to several hundred billion dollars. As leader of GE's huge bureaucracy and far-flung empire, there was a limited amount that Welch could do directly. Much of his impact came from changing strategy processes to address any weaknesses in the quality of strategic thinking in the businesses.

For example, he decided that GE's businesses needed to move quickly to take advantage of the opportunities offered by the internet. But how could he get a bunch of traditional GE managers, including himself, to think outside the box and put aside their conservative views about how a GE business should be run? (Welch confessed, 'I was afraid of (the internet), because I couldn't type.') He directed the top 600 managers to find an internal 'internet mentor', typically a younger colleague, who tutored them in web behaviour. Doing so exposed them to the power of the internet, giving them first-hand experience of what it could do.

WHEN TIME IS SHORT . . .

A particularly challenging situation for creating objective strategy is when time is short and there is no possibility to go through the typical strategy process. How do organisations in this situation avoid making flawed decisions?

Kathleen Eisenhardt of Stanford Business School has been studying strategic decision making for several decades, particularly in the fast-moving environment of Silicon Valley. Some key attributes of successful companies have been covered in this book, such as encouraging plenty of challenge and creative conflict while avoiding hostility and politics, but Eisenhardt identifies further principles for effective decision making by teams in what she describes as 'high velocity environments'.

The first is to establish strategic decision making as a *regular activity for the executive team* because it cannot be left to an annual or elaborate process. Another piece of advice is *to immerse the management team in information.* No plan survives contact with the enemy; the more uncertain the environment, the greater the value of more information. Counter-intuitively, this means that senior managers in successful fast-moving firms spend *more* time in meetings discussing information than their less successful counterparts. Practical approaches for doing this include:

▶ Adding a regular meeting (e.g. a day every month) to discuss competitors and market developments

- ▶ Setting up a management reporting system that tracks what is going on inside and outside the company, e.g. gossip in the industry, win/loss rates on recent contracts
- ▶ Making senior managers responsible for collecting particular types of data, e.g. about competitor activity or technology trends.

Unsurprisingly, another key to making rapid decisions is to *maintain a disciplined pace* to balance rigour with the need for timely decisions. To achieve this, keep the momentum up by maintaining targets for the team, keeping energy levels high and cutting off the debate when appropriate. Not only does this make the process more effective, it increases the likelihood of obtaining buy-in to the decision. If long enough is spent on debate, but not so long that everyone loses interest in the outcome, the final decision is more likely to be supported.

Techniques include:

- ▶ Developing a feel for how long a strategic decision takes in your organisation – two months? four months? How does it vary according to the nature of the decision, e.g. product launch vs. organisational change vs. acquisition? Be ready to change the timeframe if the situation proves more or less complex than expected.
- ▶ Setting a timetable for the decision, with milestones that alert you to the pace of the actual decision process.

▶ Simple testing of the emerging decision to enable you to make the decision more quickly, e.g. discuss options with trusted suppliers or customers. As the proverb goes, 'You'll never plough a field by turning it over in your mind.'

▶ If you can't develop a consensus but you need to make the decision, find another way of closing out the decision (e.g. leader decides, or voting).

THE STRATEGY TEAM

Although the main message here is to customise the decision process, most companies benefit from forming a team to develop, or support the development of, the strategy. Getting the composition, processes and reporting structure for this group right is vital but can be tricky, as you typically have to use the people who are available, whether or not they are capable of developing strategy. The effect of discussing a decision within a group can be positive, but the 'group think' phenomenon means that this is far from guaranteed. Several suggestions about how to get the group working effectively have been made in earlier sections.

There are some general principles to follow. Get a mix of perspectives – enough to eliminate blind spots or one-sided points of view. Include a few mavericks. Don't restrict your wish list to people within the organisation.

If you can't get a full complement of different personalities, try giving people different roles – such as 'guardian of the customer', 'shareholder', 'data-hound' or 'crystal ball-gazer'. Involve those responsible for implementation – especially if your strategy has to be highly adaptable to an uncertain future.

Manage the group effectively. Define how the work is to be divided up into modules. Set up meetings and shared databases to coordinate the various efforts. Establish a timetable, motivate the team, secure the required resources, monitor progress, keep the team abreast of broader organisational issues, supervise communications upwards and outwards, and celebrate success.

Some general guidance on managing project groups may be helpful if you lack experience in this area. For a quick diagnostic, consider using the DICE methodology developed by the Boston Consulting Group, which evaluates the nature of the task, the quality of the team, the support from the organisation, and the resources available.

It is also important to set up an effective governance structure. No individual or group will get it right all by themselves. It is important to set up a reporting structure to review and critique the work. Consider asking a board of advisors to make informal challenges prior to submitting your conclusions further up the hierarchy. Again, you should design the reporting structure bearing in mind the main risks to the group's objectivity.

BRINGING THE DESIGN TOGETHER

In summary, to come up with an appropriate design, use the guiding questions or thoughts on the left hand side of the following diagram to create a customised design of the various elements of the strategy process:

How to design the strategy process

Guiding thoughts or questions	Elements of the process

• What is the required ambition of the strategy?
• How precise should the strategy be?
• What are the main threats to objectivity?
  • Knowledge deficit
  • Challenge deficit
  • Consensus deficit
  • Ambition deficit
  • Pragmatism deficit
  • Problem with uncertainty
  • Short of time
• Who needs to be engaged?
	• Main activities
	• Groups to involve
	• Who should be in each group
	• How process should be managed and facilitated
	• Timetable
	• Review meetings
	• Decision-making and approval process

Note that we have not considered the implications of the last guiding thought – 'Who needs to be engaged'. This is the topic of the following chapter.

If this seems overwhelmingly complex, here are two examples of strategy process designs by way of illustration. Imagine your organisation has just emerged from hard times. You need a comprehensive review of strategy to assess the opportunities to pursue over the next few years. Your ambition is to come up with a fundamentally different strategy, without too much detail on how to implement it. There are many threats to objectivity because the current team was brought in to save the company and does not know the market well. Moreover, they tend not to look beyond a 12-month horizon. Since you have plenty of time and you feel you lack a clear picture of even the current situation, you pick a *Full Monty approach* with a comprehensive strategy process and a well-resourced strategy team, including some external consulting support.

Conversely, suppose that you face a situation in which impending changes in regulation will allow new competitors to enter the market. You understand the current situation well but decide on a 'Future Thinking' approach to explore the strategy question 'How will the situation evolve?' Your ambition is very focused: to plan how to respond within the next three months. You need a high level of detail to coordinate the activities of different parts of your organisation. Your main worry is that you don't understand what might happen next – but otherwise you are not too concerned about a lack of objectivity. You need to make a quick decision about what to do. In this context, the process might involve a small team running an initial scenarios exercise, and then a team of those involved in implementing the three month plan coming up with detailed ways of responding. The two processes are summarized on the following two pages:

Example of a Full Monty approach

Module	Sub-modules and activities	Timetable
Quick and dirty	• Initial interviews • Prepare hypotheses about answers to the strategy questions • Workshop, hypothesis revision and adjustments to process plan	• 2 weeks
Internal and external situation	• Segmentation and market and industry analysis • Competitor analysis • Analysis of cost structure • Customer interviews and evaluation of customer needs by segment • Pricing analysis • Workshop to discuss situation assessment	• 4-6 weeks
Evolution	• Market trends and analogies • Technology trends • Competitor trends • Scenarios • Workshop, including discussion of how to frame the issue • Presentation to senior team	• 4 weeks (some work done in previous module)
Issues and options	• Identification of options • Re-framing and revision to options • Option assessment • Workshop • Presentation to senior team	• 3 weeks

Example of a focused Future Thinking approach

Module	Sub-modules and activities	Timetable
Create scenarios	• Interviews with members of management team • External research and interviews (best efforts basis) • Preparation of scenarios for next 12 months • Workshop with management team	• 1-2 weeks
Action planning	• Management team to create 90 day plans • Submit plans – create integrated plan • Review at management meeting and approve • Present to Board	• 1 week
Monitoring	• On going monitoring of progress in implementing plan • Review of development of external environment • Discussion at weekly management meetings	• Ongoing

The design of a strategy process is not a mechanical activity. Use the methodology here to stimulate your thinking and to check that what you come up with makes sense. Be ready to make adjustments along the way.

INDIVIDUAL BIASES

Having designed the overall strategy process to address the *general* threats to objectivity, you should now check what *individual* biases might distort the decision process, particularly those of the most senior decision makers. Even if you have a good overall process design, personal biases remain a potential threat to objectivity.

WHO SAID IT . . .

"The brain is a wonderful organ. It starts working the moment you get up in the morning and does not stop until you get into the office."
– **Robert Frost**

Even experienced and capable decision makers can suffer from bias. There are many well publicised examples: Tony Blair and George Bush's decision to invade Iraq, Alan Greenspan's deregulation of financial markets, exposing them to meltdown, Sir Fred Goodwin, CEO of Royal Bank of Scotland, and his acquisition of ABN Amro just after Lehman Brothers had gone bankrupt and the financial markets started to nosedive.

Why do smart people make wrong decisions? The reason is related to the way the brain works, as described earlier. Our brains have evolved to interpret the world using pattern recognition and heuristics. However, under certain conditions – particularly when the situation looks familiar but is actually not – the brain can be misled.

Factors likely to lead to distortions in a decision maker's judgment include misleading experiences or prejudgments and inappropriate self-interest or attachments. To illustrate this, consider the example of Gordon Brown and his decision to run up a large deficit. As Chancellor of the Exchequer, Brown was a model of prudent management of the economy. But towards the end of his tenure he let go of the reins of the economy that he had previously held so firmly. Spending accelerated by 4.4% a year from 2001 to 2005, even as tax receipts fell. Commentators warned of the dangers. When the global financial crisis broke, the UK economy was in no shape to withstand a recession, and was soon running one of the highest budget deficits in Europe. What happened?

Why was Brown's judgment so wrong when it had previously been so right?

One explanation is that politicians may be tempted, out of *inappropriate self-interest,* to spend money to win the hearts and minds of the voters. Perhaps Brown felt an *inappropriate attachment* to the people who benefited from the increase in spending – the most disadvantaged and needy – which, while understandable, may have clouded his judgment. Another explanation is that Brown made a *misleading prior judgment* that he had banished boom and bust. He ignored the possibility that external shocks, such as a banking crisis born of risky lending practices in the US sub-prime mortgage market, might impact his stable system, sending the deficit spiralling out of control. This judgment may have been reinforced by *misleading experience.* When Labour first came to power, significant problems in public finances were forecast, but by their second year in office there was an unexpected budget surplus of over £12 billion – potentially prompting Brown to be overoptimistic about trends in public finances.

These conditions are termed 'red flags' because they provide a warning that there is a particularly high risk of an error by the decision maker. The idea here is that if you look out for potential red flags, you can spot potential biases before they affect the decision. You don't need to know for sure that someone will make a mistake (that is virtually impossible) – only that it is more likely than normal.

FINE TUNING THE PROCESS

What do you do if you spot a red flag? First, consider how it might distort the decision, then identify some extra process elements or 'safeguards' to counterbalance the distortions. Safeguards can include a wide range of interventions, process changes, people choices, analytical techniques and other mechanisms that fine-tune the strategy process, reducing the risk of a flawed decision. These additional measures counterbalance the effect of individual biases that might otherwise result in a flawed decision.

Safeguards can be grouped into four categories. The first is *experience, data, and analysis*. In business, there are many ways data can be collected and experience broadened. A discussion with a key customer, for example, can provide valuable feedback on a proposed new product. Market research can evaluate the risks of entering a new market. Consultants can be brought in, partly for their expertise and available manpower, but also because they are relatively objective.

Gordon Brown could certainly have called for an analysis of the risk of running a deficit during a boom. There was ample information available to challenge his government's spending strategies. Unfortunately, he spurned those whose reports clashed with his own ideas on spending. One civil servant commented that, 'Brown has difficulty distinguishing between disinterested advice and a knife in the back.'

The second type of safeguard is *debate and challenge*. This need not be an elaborate process; it could mean simply chatting through an issue with a friend or colleague. However, in large organisations a typical approach is to form a decision group, as discussed earlier. The difference here is that the group and the group process can be further fine-tuned to counterbalance the particular red flags of the decision maker.

WHO SAID IT . . .

"The man who gets the most satisfactory results is not always the man with the most brilliant single mind, but rather the man who can best coordinate the brains and talents of his associates."
– W. Alton Jones

Gordon Brown could have asked one of his advisers to act as a challenger or added new members to his team, but he did not welcome dissenting voices. When Brown's plans for welfare were challenged by Frank Field, Minister of Welfare Reform, Brown stopped the discussion.

Afterwards, he asked Field 'How could you disagree with me? I thought you were my friend.' Field's response was that 'It's just because I am your friend that I could disagree with you,' but this was clearly not how the challenge was perceived by Brown.

Extra *governance* is the third type of safeguard. Someone with the power and strong prejudgments so typical of leaders of many large organisations may be resistant to new analysis or challenge. In this case it may be necessary to strengthen the governance process, perhaps by setting up a special subcommittee of the board to review the proposal in detail. In the case of Gordon Brown, there was only limited direct governance. As a Prime Minister, with a large majority, he was not subject to rigorous oversight. Even his own party was unable to exert much influence on his decisions.

Monitoring is the fourth category. If all the earlier safeguards prove insufficient, it may be sensible to beef up the monitoring process – for example, by setting milestones, monitoring performance and adjusting the strategy accordingly. This can be highly effective if the results of a strategy become clear as initial investments are made – for example, when rolling out a retail network. Despite receiving copious feedback on the risks of his policies – at least from external commentators and the press – Brown either disagreed or ignored it. By the time it became clear that his spending plan was unaffordable, the full force of the financial and economic meltdown was upon him. There was little he could do.

Safeguards, if chosen well and accepted by the organisation, can reduce the risk of a flawed decision. A useful image is that of a balance, as shown below. The presence of red flags risks unbalancing the decision. To ensure balance, we add safeguards. While they do not eliminate the effect of the red flags, they do provide a counterweight. Although, as the example of Gordon Brown suggests, it can be difficult to put them in place, fortunately this is not always so. With thought and persistence it is generally possible to identify some safeguards that improve the odds of reaching an objective decision.

In choosing safeguards, the key is to pick just enough. Too many safeguards – or the wrong kind – can have a toxic effect on decision making. You can overburden the process with too much analysis, too many challenges, or

Red Flags and safeguards

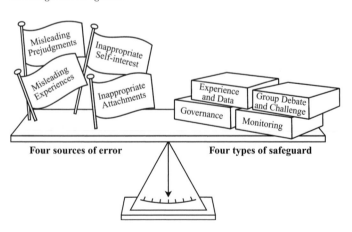

too much governance. It is easy to fall into the trap of 'pulling the tree up to see if the roots are growing'. The art is in doing just enough to counterbalance the red flags, but not too much that you overburden the decision process and de-motivate those involved. Pick as few as you need and make sure that they will work well with the decision makers involved.

Some safeguards will be ineffective or entail more negatives than positives. For example, a very aggressive challenge process can be powerful – indeed some companies develop a culture in which strong challenges are a natural part of the decision process. However, in a different organisation with different individuals a strong challenge process might engender excessive conflict or clash with a culture of decentralisation and devolution of responsibility. Overall, the fine tuning process should involve identifying any red flag conditions and selecting counterbalancing safeguards that will work in the particular context.

WHAT YOU NEED TO READ

▶ More detail on the effect of biases and what to do about them is contained in *Think Again, Why Good Leaders Make Bad Decisions and How to Keep it From Happening to You*, by Sydney Finkelstein, Jo Whitehead and Andrew Campbell, Harvard Business Press, 2008. An article summarising the book, 'Think again: how good leaders can avoid bad decisions', is published in the *Ashridge Journal*, 360, Spring 2009. For more ideas, check out www.thinkagain-book.com.

▶ *Judgment in Managerial Decision Making*, John Wiley & Sons Ltd, 2008, by Max Bazerman, is a useful guide to the effects of bias on decision making.

▶ *Predictably Irrational: The Hidden Forces That Shape Our Decisions*, Harper Collins, 2008, by Dan Ariely, is a popular book describing typical biases and their causes.

▶ *Why Great Leaders Don't Take Yes for an Answer: Managing for Conflict and Consensus*, Wharton School Publishing, 2005, by Michael Roberto, describes how to maintain the balance between objectivity and emotional engagement.

▶ The DICE methodology, which helps evaluate the ability of teams to carry out their objectives, is described at http://dice.bcg.com.

▶ A series of books and articles by Kathleen Eisenhardt explores how strategy is formulated in fast-moving environments. Examples are 'Strategy as Strategic Decision Making', *Sloan Management Review*, Spring 1999, 'Competing on the Edge', *Harvard Business Press*, 1998, with Shona Brown, and 'How Management Teams Can Have a Good Fight', with Jean L, Kahwajy, and L.J. Bourgeois III, *Harvard Business Review*, July-August, 1997.

IF YOU ONLY REMEMBER ONE THING

Design your strategy process to reflect your ambitions and produce an objective result.

CHAPTER 8
ENGAGEMENT

WHAT IT'S ALL ABOUT

- ▶ What strategy engagement is
- ▶ Why it is important
- ▶ How to engage the organisation collaboratively
- ▶ Why engagement doesn't stop at the decision
- ▶ When a more collaborative approach is important
- ▶ Leadership and culture

In previous chapters much has been said about the concepts and tools involved in strategy-making, how the process must reflect the required level of ambition and precision and enable an objective analysis of the options. However, this will not suffice to create a successful strategy; the people involved in design and implementation must be emotionally engaged. This chapter explains why and how to achieve what is called 'strategy engagement'.[1]

'Engagement' is the new buzzword: employee engagement, community engagement, stakeholder engagement. But what does engagement mean in relation to strategy, and is it more than just a fad and fashion? Is there really something important here?

WHAT STRATEGY ENGAGEMENT IS

A widely acknowledged problem in organisations is getting people to understand and act on the strategy. Senior management teams often create a strategy but then find that it is hard to get others on board.

Two different types of strategy engagement have emerged to address this problem. The first, *persuasive engagement,* seeks to get 'buy-in'. In persuasive engagement, someone

1 This chapter has been co-authored with Chris Nichols and Philippa Hardman.

WHO SAID IT . . .

"Only 5% of employees understand their company's strategy."
– **Robert Kaplan and David Norton**

already has a plan or proposition and wants everyone to agree to it and to make it happen (i.e. to become engaged in doing it). Persuasive engagement is appropriate when all strategic initiative and insight can be generated by the top management. It has a place in some situations and is still common in many organisations. It keeps strategic thinking confined to a small group, and then asks a larger group to get energised about something someone else has thought of. Trying to get buy-in means selling the idea to someone else, with the risk that it will under deliver. For this reason, and because it does nothing to improve the quality of strategic thinking, we will not consider it further.

This chapter is about *collaborative engagement*, which seeks to get people to provide input to the development of the strategy. As Nilofer Merchant puts it, it is an approach to engage all of the company 'not after the process, during the process'.

Collaborative engagement can take many forms:

- ▶ It can be a specific initiative at a time of significant organisational repositioning. This could involve getting a project team from across the business engaged in developing a strategy to enter a new market or grow through acquisition.
- ▶ It can also involve getting very large groups – even hundreds of people – to provide input into the creation of a new strategy for the organisation. Global not-for-profit healthcare organisation The Cochrane Collaboration undertook just such a process, which is described later in this chapter.
- ▶ There is also the continuous refinement of a strategy involving many people, for example, the 'Work-Out' approach developed by GE. This involves training groups in the skills required to identify and implement operational improvements to their businesses. In the early 1990s, over 200,000 GE staff participated in these sessions. In his autobiography, *Jack: What I've Learned Leading a Great Company and Great People*, CEO Jack Welch recalls a comment from a worker who told him, 'For 25 years you've paid for my hands, when you could have had my brains as well – for nothing.' While opera-

tionally focused, Work-Out played a key role in implementing GE's strategy of becoming the number one or two player in every market in which it competed.

What all the different forms of collaborative engagement have in common is that they seek to engage the participants emotionally, as well as practically and intellectually, right through the strategy process – not only during implementation or 'execution'.

WHO SAID IT . . .

"Strategy is . . . organised and purposeful collective action."
– Gary Hamel

WHY COLLABORATIVE ENGAGEMENT IS IMPORTANT

The level of engagement affects the quality of strategy because our brains focus on what is emotionally engaging. People in organisations are faced with all sorts of pressures, commitments and deadlines. Attending to strategy is only one of those pressures. Recent research in neuroscience has revealed that, to a significant extent, people decide where to focus on the basis of their emotions. For example, when faced with the choice of spending time on strategy, meeting this month's financial targets or going home a little earlier than usual, our choice will be based on what is emotionally appealing – what tickles the limbic system, which is the part of our brain responsible for registering and dealing with emotions. Moreover, the limbic system tends to operate at an unconscious level because it developed in our distant mammalian ancestors – so the choice about where to spend time can escape the auditing and critical review of the conscious brain. The brain chooses without deciding.

Emotional engagement with strategy is not too difficult to achieve if only a small group is responsible for its development, but if a large number of people are to be involved then it is a greater challenge. For this reason, large-scale collaboration is the primary focus of this chapter, although the benefits, principles and techniques also apply to a smaller group.

The first benefit of large-scale collaborative engagement is that it usually generates *more and better ideas*. When strategy is created it is common for those involved to be left with the uneasy feeling that they haven't made the best use of the minds, imaginations or collective know-how of people inside and alongside the organisation.

Good collaborative working makes the most of the amassed wisdom and day-to-day knowledge of all those involved, including those closest to the customer and products, for example in the sales team, the complaints department and the factory.

The second benefit is that it *improves the chances of the strategy being implemented effectively.* When strategy is dreamt up at the top of an organisation and then cascaded down, a gulf of understanding and ownership opens up – a phenomenon that author Nilofer Merchant calls the 'air sandwich'. In other words, there is a strategy with clear vision and direction from the top layer which people lower down then try to implement, but there is a gap between the two. Those responsible for implementing the strategy do so without really connecting the actions they are taking on a day-to-day basis with that vision or direction. However, if more people are involved, by using a collaborative process, there is a greater likelihood that a wider number will understand the overall objectives and logic of the strategy, and be motivated and able to adapt its implementation as conditions evolve.

Collaborative engagement also provides a powerful *mechanism for learning together*, developing the overall strategic capacity of the organisation and growing the capability of the next generation of leaders. By moving strategy beyond an annual ritual and into a vibrant part of organisational life, people are more alert to how it relates to their jobs. If they are confident that the mechanisms and processes exist through which their messages can be

WHO SAID IT . . .

"As long as we're eating air sandwiches we lack the way to know precisely how to do an effective job of setting direction and achieving the kind of results we need."
– Nilofer Merchant

heard and acted on, there's a greater likelihood that these 'eyes and ears' will be willing to serve as an early warning system.

Perhaps the most important benefit of collaborative engagement is that it *increases the likelihood of the organisation being able to respond to unexpected and unpredicted changes* as the strategy is implemented. A lot of writing on strategy still holds to the idea that if you plan it, it will happen. In fact, as discussed in Chapter 1, the more we understand about how strategies develop in practice, the more we see that they evolve – developing through a series of changes in circumstances and small decisions in ways that could not have been foreseen.

This doesn't mean that analysis, planning and intention have no role; far from it. These activities are important in setting direction, and the skills they require are critical for knowing how to respond to the changing situation. But it does mean that however skillfully you craft your plans you need to be alert to how a complex, connected and changing world can mess them up in unexpected ways. The more you engage people throughout the process, the more able they are to play this responsive and responsible role at all times.

HOW TO ENGAGE THE ORGANISATION COLLABORATIVELY IN CREATING OPTIONS

Irrespective of whether your strategy is created by just one or two people or by a wider group, the strategic concepts and tools used to analyse and develop strategic options are the same. What changes is the number of people involved in the conversations around the analysis. This can range from small senior or cross-functional teams of fewer than 10 people to comprehensive organisational conversations involving many.

To work out who to involve (and how many) you need to think about a number of different factors:

- ► How can we get a range of perspectives into this thinking?
- ► Who always asks the difficult questions that would help stimulate our thinking?

▶ What are the practical considerations that need to be taken into account (time, budgets, locations, technologies)?

▶ Who are the people responsible for acting on the strategic goals that emerge from this process?

If, as a result of the answers to these questions, it has been decided to include a larger number of people in the option creation process then it is best to create a number of different teams and allocate a different question or questions to each for further investigation, based on themes that have usually been defined by the board or executive team. Some teams might prioritise external inquiry while others might look at things from the inside out, thereby allowing them to challenge assumptions and 'stuck' patterns of thinking that they see within the organisation.

For example, in a strategy process for a cosmetics company, groups were established to look at issues including macro-economic and social trends over the next five years, present and future competitors, customers and shoppers, present and future consumers, brands and categories. When you are thinking about group size, typically five to eight members (including a group leader) should provide a balance between the practicalities of getting the work done and a good range of opinions in response to the questions on which you are seeking insights. While it's important to be clear about the 'big question' for each group, don't be so prescriptive about the details of every sub-question that you prevent the group from exploring something of interest that hasn't been included.

It's good to include the mavericks in your process. In deciding the composition of strategic inquiry groups during such a process in an international engineering consultancy, the MD said, 'We must make sure H is in one of the groups – he's always asking really tricky questions.' In our own research, one recipient described his role in strategy specifically as being 'an *agent provocateur* to the board. . . .' – asking the questions that the CEO wished he hadn't. It may be difficult to handle the questions that result, yet these dissident voices often provide vital insight into opportunities and risks in both the internal and external environments.

PRACTICAL TIPS ON GENERATING ENGAGEMENT

Practical considerations include thinking about how much time and budget you have. If the group is very large, this may not permit a face-to-face encounter but there are many virtual ways of gathering input (such as online meeting platforms). It is possible to involve large groups of people in quite a short timeframe, so long as the process is well thought through and creatively designed.

As an illustration, consider The Cochrane Collaboration, founded in 1993 as an independent, not-for-profit organisation of over 28,000 contributors from more than 100 countries and dedicated to promoting evidence-based healthcare by making independent evaluations of current medical and health research available worldwide. With so many volunteers so widely spread, how could they be engaged in a review of the organisation's strategy? Seven inquiry dialogues were set up, with a series of interviews by phone and intranet surveys open to any contributor to The Collaboration which, when combined with an interactive exhibition space at their annual conference, resulted in over 3,000 people inputting to the strategic intent.

If there are several groups, all working on different issues, it is important that they not be exclusive and closed, but porous and inviting. Make sure that your work groups know they can invite others to share their insight into their area of inquiry. In the cosmetics company mentioned previously, the macro-economic team used an external agency to provide more in-depth information about expected societal trends, while the competitor team interviewed new hires recruited from competitor organisations to supplement data from desk research.

SHARING FINDINGS

If many people are involved then there must be a particular emphasis on communication. Each group needs to know something about the findings of the others. Groups should be encouraged to talk to each other if they discover something that might be useful to another group or believe they have overlaps in their thinking. Collaborative engagement means just that!

Given the mix of backgrounds of the people involved, forms of communication should not be restricted to those typical of strategy processes in large companies. If you think about the outputs of strategy work done in your organisation, what comes to mind? Almost certainly it will be some kind of report – most likely presented as a series of PowerPoint slides. But there are other ways of representing strategic exploration, from the traditional slideshow to poster exhibitions, photo montages, stories, poems and 'street theatre' productions. The following example shown is based on one produced by a company reviewing its five year strategy. Out of five inquiry groups set up by the Board, one was tasked with assessing market position. Each group was asked to bring their findings to a one-day workshop in a way that could be shared and added to by others attending. The market position group put their thinking (predominantly hand drawn) onto a large piece of brown paper. It was spread out on a table at the workshop and, through the course of the day, people stood around it, discussing and annotating the outputs.

The purpose of using a range of creative ways of representing data is not just to make the process interesting. Different ways of exploring and seeing data reveal new

Creative communication

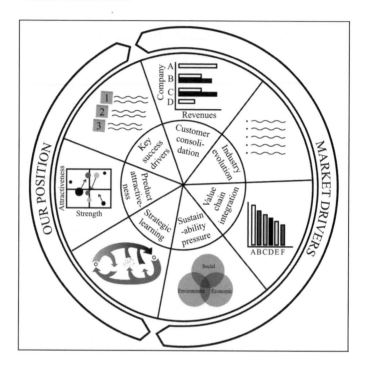

perspectives. A picture, a collage or a story can provide a different insight into the nature of a problem, a challenge or an opportunity.

These approaches can later be adapted to illustrate and communicate the strategic story to other parts of the organisation. For example, once further changes had been incorporated, the exhibit shown above was drawn up by the in-house graphics team. It was then used as part of the presentation to the Board and, from there, across the rest of the organisation as a way of telling the strategic story and the rationale for decisions made.

Communications also need to flow up the hierarchy. Throughout this process, the board or executive team keeps a watching brief over the inquiry work groups, deliberately avoiding giving their views on content, but usefully asking probing questions. In the cosmetics company, each team had a board sponsor who briefed the team on what was required at the beginning of the process, then met twice with the team leader during the six weeks they were collating and making sense of data. At those meetings, the board sponsors were given a brief update on progress, after which they asked questions to ensure sufficient depth and rigour was being applied (e.g. 'How are you going to investigate competitor X? What impact will conscience-led shoppers have on us in the future?').

ENGAGING THE ORGANISATION IN CHOOSING AN OPTION

A comment often made by senior managers is that 'Engagement sounds fine, but if we involve more people then they'll think that means they also have a decision-making vote.' This is not the case. Organisations are rarely constituted as democracies. One of the reasons that senior people get paid more is because they have to take decisions and are legally accountable for the decisions they take. Nonetheless, there is a strong case to be made for engaging others in the decision-making process, not as decision-makers but to keep the executive group as well informed as possible, to act as a critical friend or devil's advocate, or to challenge 'stuck thinking' within the senior group.

You can use people new to the strategy conversation, thereby widening the organisation engagement further,

WHO YOU NEED TO KNOW
Ron Heifetz

Ron Heifetz is a leadership expert and a graduate of Columbia University, Harvard Medical School and the Kennedy School, where he is currently the King Hussein bin Talal Senior Lecturer in Public Leadership. He is also a physician and cellist.

Heifetz distinguishes between technical tasks and adaptive challenges. Sometimes a strategic challenge is genuinely the former: familiar ground where existing experience and expertise can provide the answer. But usually strategy is more complex than this, and innovation in product, service or organisation is called for. Here, Heifetz argues, it is wrong for top leaders to claim expertise – a more collective intelligence and learning effort is needed. He argues that top leaders have to 'give the work back to the people'.

The role of the leader is not to be the font of all strategic knowledge, but to create the space in which teams can explore, enquire and create solutions and approaches for a new future. Top leaders can't deliver it alone, so it's unwise to exclude the people who have to do the work from the process of exploring the solutions needed. Heifetz talks about the role of leaders as being to invite and support teams in engaging deeply in strategic challenges and the strategic learning that goes along with them.

261

albeit with the downside that they will need to be engaged in the thinking that has already taken place (which may have a time implication). Alternatively, you can use those already in place from previous work.

With the cosmetics company, the team leaders were tasked to examine all the data and then act as a 'shadow board' to address the questions – 'On the basis of what you've seen, what are the most significant strategic issues we face and how should we as an organisation best respond to them?' Having done this, the shadow board met the main board to present their findings, which were taken into account in the latter's deliberations. The board was not bound by their suggestions, yet the additional insights helped to sharpen their thinking before they made their final decisions.

Such diversity is useful. It encourages issues and options to be seen 'through multiple lenses', minimising the problem of group think. This is especially so if the groups include divergent perspectives. It is, for example, possible to include key stakeholders such as suppliers, selected customers, investor groups and trade bodies in this process. (There is no reason that your engagement should stop at the company gate). Where issues are too sensitive to invite external parties into the room, it can be very powerful and creative to role-play the position of such parties in the options' selection and evaluation process. Again, this tends to enrich the conversation and encourage decisions to be taken having looked from more diverse angles than the more familiar ones.

WHO YOU NEED TO KNOW
Gary Hamel

Gary Hamel is one of the world's most provocative business writers and speakers, and is highly sought after as an advisor and inspirer. A founder and chairman of Strategos, and Visiting Professor of Strategic and International Management at the London Business School, he has authored 15 articles published in the Harvard Business Review, the benchmark of success for a management writer.

Hamel's interests have roamed widely over the years, but have a common theme – the mobilisation of capabilities to achieve competitive success. His more recent thinking has focused on a capability of particular relevance to how strategy is developed – 'human imagination and initiative' – and its ability to help an organisation innovate and adapt to the rapidly changing business environment. He dreams of organisations where '. . . the renegades always trump the reactionaries'.

Hamel seeks to break the 'ongoing tension between creativity and organisation', encouraging managers to find ways to delegate more decision making down the hierarchy. He urges organisations to loosen the shackles that constrain their employees so that they can be engaged in the task of reshaping, building and directing their organisations. This approach is aligned with the ideas presented in this chapter.

As you might imagine, opinion is divided on the validity of Hamel's views. He is criticised by some for being impractical. What is generally agreed is that he has put his finger on a problem that many large organisations would love to solve. The question then is: Has Hamel provided a solution? In his own words, 'My goal . . . was not to predict the future of management, but to help you invent it.'

Hamel and his co-author C.K. Prahalad have made other important contributions to strategic thinking, including the importance of strategic intent in motivating an organisation, and the development of capabilities and core competencies to build competitive advantage, even against entrenched competitors.

There are situations, of course, in which the situation is more democratic, such as where an organisation operates as a cooperative, collaborative or is employee owned. But even here decision-making authority is usually vested in a board or other executive group, perhaps with employee directors. Equally, there are situations when broadening participation in the decision-making process is much less appropriate. For example, when deciding on a market-sensitive acquisition where confidentiality is key, decision-making conversations rightly remain closely held by the most senior individuals in the organisation.

WHY ENGAGEMENT DOESN'T STOP AT THE DECISION

This is not a book about strategy implementation, so why include this section?

In traditional strategy thinking, the start of implementation is sometimes seen as the end of the 'strategy' process. The thinking and decision making are done and it is time to turn decisions into action. But, as described earlier, the strategy written down is virtually never the same as the strategy that actually develops over time. Unforeseeable events occur, competitors do unexpected things, new entrants arrive and circumstances change. The plans do not unfold as anticipated. Even your own colleagues can come up with ways of satisfying customers that you never thought of . . . and they work! So these become part of the strategy too. As Henry Mintzberg said, strategy grows more like weeds than cultivated prize tomatoes.

For this reason, the process of engagement does not finish with the roll-out of the initial strategy. The awareness, attention and learning ability of the organisation needs to be harnessed in order to allow the strategic actions to be refined as the strategy adapts to changing circumstances. The more people are primed to act as the nerve endings of the organisation, noticing the tiny signals that this or that is happening, the more the organisation is able to react. It can still follow its plan, but does so intelligently and flexibly in an uncertain world.

The more widely the strategy is understood throughout the organisation, the more people are able to use their awareness and intelligence to adapt it as needed. They are also more alert to strategically important events and developments and bring these swiftly to the attention of the senior team. So a critical first step is to communicate your strategy effectively. But, despite its importance, there are many organisations in which most of its members are unsure what the strategy is.

Partly this is the age old problem of communicating *any* consistent message across all but the smallest organisations. But the problem is often compounded by the strategy being described in a way that is fuzzy and generic. The key is to boil the strategy down to something very simple, but also very distinctive.

A useful tool to use to develop your message is the strategy triangle – discussed in Chapter 2. This is composed of the three elements that your communication needs to include: The objectives of the strategy, the opportunities it is targeting and the capabilities that will be used.

The description of the objective can include both the specific objective of the strategy – such as achieving the number one spot in the market – as well as how that supports the organisation's broader purpose and mission. The opportunity, or scope of the strategy, should make clear the boundaries of the strategy – what you won't do as well as what you will. The capabilities should be expressed as the distinctive way in which you will achieve your objectives – rather than a bland list of generic ideas such as 'excellence', 'people' or 'persistence'. Instead, state the characteristics that differentiate your approach from that of other organisations – your distinctive competitive advantage.

Distinctiveness is critical. Too many strategy statements could be used by a different organisation without anyone noticing! Test the distinctiveness of your communication by asking how each element of the communication differs from that of your competitors.

Another objective is to ensure a good flow of information about how the strategy is progressing. There are a number of ways to do this:

▶ Making sure that there are *feedback loops* built into every part of the organisation to report back on the progress of the strategy – what's working, what's not, what people are noticing, what's actually happening. This may mean specific meetings are set up to review the strategy (monthly, quarterly) or, perhaps more pragmatically, an agenda item at regular team/departmental/divisional meetings. The point is that it's an ongoing process that operates at all times in the life of the organisation. At one major UK charity, a specific aim of regular team meetings is to provide a two-way flow of information about the strategy as it takes shape on the ground.

▶ Formalising the skill and capability of strategic thinking by including it in *competency and appraisal processes*. If you pay the right kind of attention to this behaviour, you will get more of it. It's not just about recognition in the form of pay and advancement, it's also about what behaviours get praised, talked about and written up in the company newsletter.

▶ Encouraging awareness of the place of learning and feedback in the strategic process through the way *senior managers demonstrate their own willingness to learn* from what's happening. This also means an acknowledgement from such individuals (overtly or otherwise) that they cannot know everything that is going on in the organisation, and recognising the importance of strategic intelligence wherever it comes from. Without this type of senior sponsorship and involvement, strategic learning will not flourish in your organisation.

To hone this strategic intelligence it is important to develop the strategic capability of those in teams responsible for turning ideas into action. Again, this can be done in a number of ways:

▶ Start by *developing awareness of the basic strategic tools and models* used in your organisation's thinking. Some of the models introduced earlier in this book may already be in use. Familiarity with such tools and models is important – especially learning not to be baffled by the science (or apparent magic) of strategy. The tools are there to help you have a more focused conversation, to ask better questions in a complex world.

▶ A further step in growing strategic capability is to *encourage people to develop a 'strategic perspective'*. This involves learning to spot potential connections between events (internal and external) and the organisation's strategic intentions. It means that, when you read the press, watch the TV news, or stumble across something interesting on the web, you think about the strategic consequences for your part of the business. It grows out of curiosity and is fed by conversations that come from having your eyes and ears open to what in the world might impact you, to your cost or advantage. This perspective can be encouraged through practice and by noticing that there are genuinely many ways to see, understand and think creatively. A good way of illustrating this comes from the cosmetics company. At the end of the options datagathering process, the Director of Consumer Insights commented, 'I realise that I should be thinking in this way almost all of the time.'

It's by paying attention to what's really happening that your organisation can respond to things that don't work out as you expected and exploit new opportunities that emerge that were never considered possible when the strategic intent was first worked up.

WHEN A MORE COLLABORATIVE APPROACH IS IMPORTANT

Sometimes a strategic decision is totally within the leader's or top team's expertise, and needs no exploring. In such circumstances it makes no sense to use a more collaborative approach. Simply own your expertise and take the decision. (You may of course want to think about how best to engage people in understanding the decision – that is the sphere of persuasive engagement and is about how well you tell the story – but the point is, you don't need a larger group to help you explore it). Never engage people in collaborative strategy-making when you have already made up your mind about the answer; it just makes them cynical and is bad practice.

But sometimes a strategic situation is beyond the expertise or experience of anyone – including senior managers and expert consultants. No single person can bring certainty; the organisation must draw on its collective intelligence, its ability to learn and experiment. It is in this context that the most developed forms of collaborative engagement become vital.

Another time to involve a broad group is when the implementation task is particularly challenging. For example, if it requires a detailed understanding of the rationale for the strategy, a deep commitment to implementation, a high degree of creative adaptation of the strategy, or a large pool of people with a strategic mindset, then involving many people can be essential.

LEADERSHIP AND CULTURE

Two themes run through these last three chapters on the strategy process, each worth a brief mention – although either could be the topic of a whole book.

The first is the role of leadership in designing, shaping and managing the strategy process. This is a two-way street. The leader needs to adapt to suit the process, and the process often needs to be designed to suit the leader. An important choice that leaders must make is the extent to which they roll their sleeves up and get involved in the task vs. managing the decision process at a distance. Both approaches are classic responsibilities of a leader and it is tempting to do some of each, but be careful not to think that you can handle both without risking a loss of either objectivity or careful management of the process.

If the focus is on managing the process, many of the more detailed activities described earlier can be delegated to a team leader, although they will require some senior involvement and oversight. A key role is to ensure that healthy conflict and debate is fostered without it spilling over into personal battles or acrimony. Depending on the group, this may be an easy or near impossible task. Any project leader whom you appoint may need assistance.

Another important role where you can help is to pace the overall effort and decide when to open it up to more ideas, and when to bring it to focus and closure. Strategy development is difficult and teams may get lost without some external guidance.

One final responsibility for leaders is to acknowledge that they themselves may be a major source of bias. They should assume that is the case and be open to, or encourage, safeguards that prevent them leading the strategy astray. Easy in principle – rare in practice!

The other theme running through these chapters is that different organisations have different cultures. Hence a particular style of strategy-making can be pleasure for one organisation and poison for another. An important issue, drawing on a framework developed by Rob Goffee and Gareth Jones, is how sociable your organisation is. The more sociable, the broader the debate can be – as everyone will want to contribute. However, you are also in more danger of falling into the 'group think' trap. Less sociable organisations will find it easy to set up a project team, but difficult to engage the entire organisation.

Another dimension on which cultures vary is what Goffee and Jones describe as 'solidarity' – the degree to which individuals agree to particular goals and ways of working. An organisation with a high level of solidarity works like an effective machine – where things are done using particular operating procedures. In such an environment, creating strategy will be welcomed if it is an accepted way of operating (think of a high-tech business that is continually re-designing its strategy) – but rejected if it is seen as a threat to or deviation from standard ways of operating (imagine trying to get a bunch of senior doctors to engage in a strategy process challenging the way they run their hospital department).

You probably understand intuitively that any process will be easier to operate if it fits the existing culture – but make sure that you also give it some conscious thought and debate.

WHAT YOU NEED TO READ

► Nilofer Merchant's *The New How* provides a guide to collaborative strategy-making. More information is at *http://the-new-how.com*.

► Chapter 18 of Ralph Stacey's *Strategic Management and Organisational Dynamics*, FT Prentice Hall, 2002, is a provocative challenge to orthodox management thinking and includes helpful suggestions for leaders.

► Ron Heifetz's classic *Leadership Without Easy Answers*, Harvard University Press, 1998, or his article 'The Work of Leadership' (written with Don Laurie, *Harvard Business Review*, Jan-Feb 1997) provide thoughts on leading strategy development.

► Ideas on creating the conditions for good group work can be found in Lynda Gratton's *Hot Spots: Why Some Companies Buzz with Energy and Some Don't*, FT Prentice Hall, 2007, or Dorothy Leonard and Walter Swap's *When Sparks Fly*, Harvard Business Press, 1999, or on Google Books.

▶ Teresa Amabile's Harvard Business Review article *How to Kill Creativity* is a handy summary of her many years of researching creative groups.

▶ *The Art of Action*, Nicholas Brealey Publishing, 2011, by Stephen Bungay provides more ideas on the links between strategy-making and implementation.

▶ Rob Goffee and Gareth Jones' *The Character of a Corporation*, Profile Books, 2003, provides a useful introduction to organisational cultures.

IF YOU ONLY REMEMBER ONE THING

Involve a larger group in developing strategy if you need more ideas or stronger implementation.

ON YOUR WAY

In a fast-moving world, everyone needs to know something about strategy – even if only to decide where to focus when carrying out their day to day responsibilities. This book has described how to think through a strategy and provides a basis for developing the knowhow required to think strategically.

Strategy making is both simple and challenging. All you need to do is answer a few basic questions. It's coming up with the answers, which is the tricky bit. Fortunately there are aids to guide your thinking. Creating strategy is always a creative act but, like any artist, you can improve your craft – there are concepts and tools to help you structure your thought process.

And you are not alone. By involving a good mix of people in the right process you can share expertise and hone your arguments. Strategy making is the art of bringing all these components together – using the concepts, tools, people and process in a way that is customised to your situation.

However, the answers are only the start – the success of any strategy depends not just on how you make it, but how you *implement* it.

If you follow the approach to designing strategy suggested here you will be well on the way to a successful outcome. You will have thought ahead, creating a strategy that will be effective when the rubber hits the road. You will have built commitment to the strategy by engaging the implementers in the process. You will have communicated your strategy effectively and developed the strategic intelligence of your organisation. Now you must select the right way of rolling out the strategy.

The way you put your strategy in place depends on the level of uncertainty and unpredictability that the strategy has to deal with. The less certain you are, the more flexible your approach should be.

If you know your suggested plan is 'the one and only' then all you need to do is map out the tasks, responsibilities and milestones in a structured and detailed fashion.

On the other hand, if the pathway is a bit less predictable, then you'll need to build in opportunities to intervene and adapt the strategy as it develops. You'll need to communicate faster and more often about what is going on

– both with the implementation and the external situation. You'll need to be able to re-plan and re-issue your plans.

Sometimes, though, things are even more uncertain. When the environment is highly unpredictable and a lot of different expertise is required to make things happen, you need to be able to loosen your grip on the reins, allowing the strategy to adapt to the evolving situation.

The solution, in such circumstances, is to set clear objectives and constraints, but otherwise to not be too prescriptive. Having set these broad objectives, ask for more detailed plans to be developed by the next layer down in the organisation. Review and comment on the plans, but let those who have created the plans implement and adapt them to emerging conditions.

Those implementing the strategy should come back to you only if they need to change the objective or constraints, or get more resources. This approach is what author Stephen Bungay describes as 'directed opportunism' – the do-ers are encouraged to seize opportunities so long as they reflect the objectives and constraints that they have been given. You can then spend the time you have available to focus on the most critical areas where you can add the most value. Leave the rest to your team to implement.

To make this approach work, you have to be able to trust those you are delegating too. Adequate training, teamwork and a shared commitment to the success of the strategy are a pre-condition. That is why this approach is hard to pull off – but powerful when it happens.

How to design a strategy is not a skill you learn solely from a book. It comes from an iterative process of learning, doing and reflecting. So – once you have read this book you will need to get some practice! You can start with the book's website, www.whatyouneedtoknowaboutstrategy. com which has worked case examples and suggestions for further reading.

Consult magazines, newspapers and books to read about other organisations and strategists. Try and work out how they have answered the strategic questions – so that you can learn from what others have done successfully or unsuccessfully. Ask those around you what they think the strategy of your organisation is – or what the strategies are of your competitors. Investigate what strategies were developed in the past and how they have performed when implemented. Read other books about strategy. Get involved, where you can, in creating new strategies for your own organisation.

This book provides a framework of questions and insights to help you become a better strategist. If you use it and apply it you will have started on the cycle of learning and doing. Get out there and get going!

ACKNOWLEDGEMENTS

In writing this book I have been grateful for the ideas, advice and comments of many people, including Christoph Burger, Stephen Bungay, Andrew Campbell, Martin Essayan, Franziska Frank, Rob Goffee, Mike Goold, Barbara Minto, Thedoore Modis, Phil Renshaw, Martin Richardson, Toby Roe, David Sadtler, Tony Sheehan and Tom Wilkinson. Thanks also to the many colleagues at the Boston Consulting Group and London Business School who set me on my strategy pathway.

Also many thanks to Angela Munro for her support on the website, Michelle Moore and her team and Jenny Ng for help on the exhibits, Annie Brakx and Hazel Hamelin who edited assiduously and Ellen Hallsworth my publisher.

Particular thanks go to my co-authors for Chapter 8, Philippa Hardman and Chris Nichols.

The biggest help has come from all the MBA and executive course attendees that I have had the pleasure of working with. I would love to think that you have learned as much from me as I have from you.

The greatest strategic challenge in my life, as well as its greatest pleasure, has been having a family – so I dedicate this book to my wonderful boys, Charlie, Tom and Ben.

INDEX

Symbols
5 Whys 151, 171, 181,
   204
7S framework 84
Henderson, Bruce 79

A
Ansoff matrix 160
Apple 6–10, 16, 17, 19, 26,
   73, 77, 91, 97, 98, 133,
   163, 166, 179, 180, 194
Ashridge Mission
   Diamond 98, 99

B
BCG 79–81, 93, 105, 243
Best practices 211
Blue Ocean Strategy 110

Bounded rationality 218
British Airways 94, 104

C
China 43, 44, 46, 47, 50, 51,
   102, 133
Christensen, Clayton 132
Churchill, Winston 107
Cisco 93
Coca Cola 22, 91, 98
Competitive advantage
   22–24, 41, 50, 59, 60, 71,
   72, 77, 78, 80, 86–88, 90,
   94, 95, 97, 98, 104–106,
   110, 122, 123, 172–175,
   188, 264, 267
Customer value
   proposition 72, 76

D

Data 22, 72, 75, 88, 89, 106,
107, 127–129, 135, 174,
191, 196, 201, 204, 210,
215, 221, 227, 229, 237,
256, 257, 259, 262, 270

Deconstruction 181

Deconstruction 133

Definition 122, 123, 169

Definition of 105

De Gaulle, Charles 86

Deming, Edwards 74

Direct Line 42

Disruptive technologies 132,
143

E

Epson 28

Evaluating 20, 27, 75, 88, 90,
92, 119, 145, 147, 148, 172,
175, 176, 178, 197, 219

External environment 15,
16, 26, 27, 38, 41, 70, 122,
140, 205, 212

F

Fairtrade 74

Financial metrics 107

Five forces 24, 49, 56, 59, 60,
63, 64, 66, 67, 69, 159

Framing 145, 147–151, 153,
171, 178–180, 195, 196, 210

G

GE matrix 104

Generating new 145, 168

Generating new frames 145,
150, 152

Google 69, 74, 78, 190, 275

Grant, Robert 35, 69, 110,
142

Growth-Share Matrix 80

H

Hamel, Gary 85

Harvard Business Review 34,
69, 142, 243, 263, 274,
275

Harvard Business School 30,
58, 79, 110, 132, 181, 182,
187, 189

Henderson, Bruce 20

Hewlett Packard 28, 186

Honda 11, 15–17, 19, 82, 83,
132

How to create 148, 149, 153,
182

I

Implementation 156, 178,
185, 213, 214, 229, 246,
249, 251, 265, 271, 275,
279

Importance of 4, 14, 37, 76,
77, 110, 148, 264, 269

Improving objectivity 209,
220

Industry life cycle 24, 132,
142

In Search of Excellence 84

Intuition 21, 117, 122, 139,
189

J
Jobs, Steve 7, 8

K
Kennedy, John 125
Key success factors 24
Kiechel 35, 110
Koch, Richard 34, 69, 111

L
Lehman Brothers 7, 18, 235

M
Macro environment 128
McDonald's 74
McKinsey 30, 81, 83, 84, 93, 104, 140, 142
Merrill Lynch 10
Minto Pyramid Principle 29, 30, 221
Mintzberg, Henry 79, 121
Mission and Objectives 71, 73, 98, 111
Moët & Chandon 22, 23
Motorcycle industry 11, 19, 21
Motorola 11, 18, 21, 166
Multiple horizons 160

N
Narrowing down 147, 152
Nature of 92, 102, 122, 128, 177, 195, 196, 198, 206, 216, 221, 227, 229, 258

Niels Bohr 32
Nokia 11, 77

O
Objectives 73, 102, 103, 106, 146, 150, 154–156, 171, 243, 251, 267, 279
Operational metrics 109
Options 17, 18, 143, 145–158, 160, 161, 164–168, 171–174, 176, 177–180, 185, 189, 193–197, 204, 205, 210, 212, 220, 223, 228, 246, 253, 262, 270
Overall approaches to 116
Oxfam 74

P
People 12, 13, 21, 25, 26, 35, 42, 64, 72, 75, 93, 99, 100, 121, 126, 137, 148, 159, 161, 168, 180, 185, 193, 194, 209, 210, 216–224, 228, 229, 235–237, 246–248, 250, 251, 253–257, 259–261, 266–269, 271, 277, 278, 281
Performance 71–73, 106–111, 177, 239
PESTLE 24, 66–68, 128, 129
Peters, Tom 83
Porter, Michael 39, 40, 58, 69, 79, 84, 97
Portfolio matrices 24
Positional advantage 90, 92

Prioritising 113, 137, 178, 197

R
Red flags 236, 238, 240, 241
Rentokil 217
Risk/return 172, 176, 178
Ryanair 76, 78

S
Safeguards 237, 239, 240, 241, 273
Scenarios 124–126, 165, 174, 177, 191, 193, 194, 224, 231
Segmentation 41, 42, 44–47, 49, 122, 158, 172
Seneca 117, 155
Shell 142, 193
Sources of 16, 41, 50, 60, 70, 74, 78, 85, 90–92, 96, 97, 110, 114, 131, 157, 159, 195, 220
South Africa 193
Southwest Airlines 93
Stakeholder analysis 98, 101
Stalk, George 81, 82
Strategic concept 22
Strategic metrics 108
Strategy 4, 6, 7, 14, 15, 23, 32, 34, 35, 59, 69, 77, 79, 81–83, 85, 86, 91, 98–100, 102, 104–107, 109–111, 114, 115, 119, 121, 122, 125, 126, 135, 137–139, 142, 143, 147, 152–154, 156–158, 160, 163, 164, 166, 167, 169–174, 176, 177, 179–191, 194, 196–202, 204–207, 209–214, 216, 217, 220–226, 228–231, 234, 237, 239, 243, 245–257, 260, 261, 263, 265–269, 271–275, 277–281
Strategy matrix 105, 106
Strategy process 25, 26, 28, 48
Strategy questions 3, 4, 14, 19, 25, 27
Strategy tools 24, 25
Strategy Triangle 102–104, 106
Substitution curves 130, 131
Sull, Don 85, 140, 142
Summarising 71, 102, 104, 113, 171, 202, 242
SWOT 24, 102, 188
Systems thinking 110

T
Taleb, Nassim 120
Tesco 32, 92, 114, 115, 159, 200, 201
The power of 145, 148, 149, 168, 194, 225
Toyota 41, 45, 79, 82, 161, 181

U
Uncertainty 114–116, 119, 121, 123, 124, 126, 128,

129, 134, 138, 140, 142,
143, 164, 174, 181, 182,
184, 185, 205, 209, 213,
219, 223, 224, 278
Unilever 93, 167, 169

V
Value chain 24, 45–48, 59,
91, 97, 159
Value curve 76, 159
Value innovation 74

Value tree 107, 108
Volkswagen 41, 43, 45, 48

W
Welch, Jack 34
Who, What, How
analysis 160

Y
Youth Hostel Association
99